Teaching
Springboard
Diving

Teaching Springboard Diving

ANNE ROSS FAIRBANKS

Illustrated by Gil Evans and Craig Kavafes

Prentice-Hall Inc., Englewood Cliffs, N. J. 1963

PRENTICE-HALL INTERNATIONAL, INC., *London*
PRENTICE-HALL OF AUSTRALIA, PTY., LTD., *Sydney*
PRENTICE-HALL OF CANADA, LTD., *Toronto*
PRENTICE-HALL FRANCE, S.A.R.L., *Paris*
PRENTICE-HALL OF JAPAN, INC., *Tokyo*
PRENTICE-HALL DE MEXICO, S.A., *Mexico City*

Library of Congress Catalog Card Number 63–11100

Printed in the United States of America 89409—C

Foreword

One of the fundamental needs in the development of a sporting skill is the devotion of those who have benefited from the sport toward the teaching and training of others.

During the thirty or more years in which I have competed or served as an administrator of Fancy Diving, I have been singularly impressed by the genuine and thorough dedication of divers toward each other. It is a sport, in the finest sense of the word, where the unselfish efforts of champions have been directed constantly toward guiding those who ultimately will succeed them.

It is not unusual, therefore, that a distinguished American diving champion should collaborate with another outstanding diver and artist, to produce this book, dedicated to teaching diving. For here is the rare combination of athlete and teacher, writer and artist, whose joint aim is to improve the teaching techniques of a truly significant sport.

R. Jackson Smith,
U. S. A. Representative and
Vice-Chairman of the
International Diving Committee

January 1962

Preface

Teaching Springboard Diving is for beginning teachers—starting with the first process of getting in head first and continuing to the low board. The dive descriptions and coaching points are all for lowboard diving, with the exception of Chapter 15.

The book is planned for teachers beginning to teach diving, whether they are students in training in physical education or those already installed in aquatics and suddenly faced with the prospect of teaching diving. Diving is a specialty for which there is rarely time in aquatics methods courses. It is brushed over lightly and is taught almost always by people who themselves are not too familiar with diving. Even if one is a diving expert, how much can be accomplished in a one- or two-hour session? This manuscript is a result of many workshops and clinics which I have conducted at colleges, teacher training institutions, and clubs in the past fifteen years. It is partly the result of repeated questions and confusions about teaching diving which I find everywhere.

Although there are diving books available that are good from the competitive coaching standpoint, it has been my feeling that a basic diving book is needed. I am trying to fill a gap here, to put in many little pieces of information which I have not seen in print. I have had experience in diving from the performer's standpoint in competition and as a professional diver, and have also had a background of teaching in the whole area of physical education as well as in aquatics. I am trying to contribute something here from both sides of the picture: as a diver and as a diving teacher.

An effort has been made to keep the material strictly to diving fundamentals for the educational situation, with a minimum of emphasis on big competition and advanced coaching. In my own teaching in colleges and clubs, I know how rarely one really has the opportunity to "develop" a top diver. The average teacher keeps getting new beginners and half-taught intermediates. Yet we all know that the basic material is very essential for the top diver as well as for the novice, and I would hope that advanced divers might glean some helpful information here too.

A word of appreciation must go to my own teacher, Madeline "Buddy" Karson, who taught me all I knew as a diver from the age of twelve through several national championships a half dozen years later; to the moral support of understanding and encouraging parents; and to many diving students who suffered through my growing pains in teaching.

In putting together this book I would like to thank the Amy Morris Homans Fellowship Award Committee of Wellesley College for their grant toward cost of illustration. To my illustrator, co-diver, and friend, Gil Evans, thanks for much patience and skill.

ANNE ROSS FAIRBANKS

Contents

I

Philosophy of Teaching Diving

Diving is a highly specialized aquatic sport that utilizes principles of physics and body mechanics to attain patterns of bodily flight as the diver rises and descends through the air into a body of water. A light plunge from the edge of a pool for the simple purpose of getting in to swim may be considered a dive as well as a three-second flight with complex revolutions from a ten meter platform. It may be a physical position held momentarily in the air and framing an image of grace and line in the spectator's eye, or it may consist of a breathtaking series of turns and twists. Either type of dive, that is, the dive which emphasizes form, or the dive which emphasizes aerial acrobatics, can be profoundly effective. Ease of performance is a measure of perfection, and the more effortless it appears, the more a dive can be appreciated.

There is an intangible poignancy about beautiful physical performance in diving, as well as in dancing or skating or swimming or even walking. Over and above the effects of smooth, efficient mechanics, there are added the human elements of unique style, personality, sense of achievement, and the performer's own cognizance of the skill and action he is at once directing, enacting, visualizing, and evaluating. All of this communicates the excitement and enhances the beauty of the few seconds of movement we call a dive.

The diver feels his movement as the center of action. He *is* the picture he is painting. So he must learn to feel his own motion and, at the same time, learn to judge very finely the meaning of what he feels. Always he must be able to picture in his mind what he looks like in the eye of a viewer. It is quite true that a diver visualizes the dive before he performs it, and this takes many years of constant adjusting and correcting the inner and outer visualization to what is true, what is intended, and what is attained.

The teacher of diving must impart to his student the methods of performing a dive from the point of view of being *inside* that dive, and also get across what it looks like from the *outside*. The hope is that the diver will bring the two aspects closer and closer together. When he succeeds in a real synthesis, this may or may not mean that he has become an excellent diver, but he can then feel kinesthetically what he is doing and also correctly visualize his action as he does it. It may be incorrect or inefficient, but he knows exactly where he stands physically and intellectually. Only then can the student correct and perfect his actions.

All of these somewhat theoretical statements are to tell the diving teacher that he must get "inside" the student to succeed in teaching good diving. He must work and work to make the student understand what is happening. Diving cannot be taught by command and obedience. There must be understanding and honest comprehension. In practical terms this means teaching by questions: What did it *feel* like? Did you feel any *pressure* as you entered the water? Where? Were your eyes open? What did you see? Resist the impulse to *tell* the student that his legs went over —ask, and let the student give you the answer. Only then will he begin to work in terms of conscious awareness of his own movement *as it happens*. Only then will he be able to change this movement as desired.

This principle refers not only to so-called "fancy" diving; it applies to all phases of diving from beginning to advanced stages and, in fact, to all teaching of physical motion.

An essential quality needed in a good teacher of diving is the ability to observe movement, both as a total sequence of action and in its separate phases. One must have the ability to catch slight changes or aberrations in rhythm, sound of the feet, angle, balance, and tension in the diver; and from these to pinpoint the fault which is causing an incorrect result. This ability to weigh and judge is based on a fineness of perception in the teacher. There is nothing magic or specialized about it. It comes with practice, with continuous watching and evaluating and experimenting. The diver and the teacher can help each other—one inside the dive, the other outside. Together they try to find the cause and effect.

Complexity in diving begins with the springboard. So many physical laws enter into the control of this lever and its human projectile: the basic principle of the fulcrum, the shifting relationship of the diver to gravity, and all the individual differences in weight, body structure, and flexibility. Psychological factors add to the complexity of physical factors. They include temperament, the influences of other learned physical skills, past experience in diving, conceit, modesty, courage, fear, and rapport with the teacher. The weather itself or the lighting in the pool may be serious factors in diving. The teacher must be aware of these factors, yet must sort out the vital point of emphasis from each and give his instructions a single direction at a time. Above all he must not make diving hypochondriacs out of his students—ones who make exacting demands of their diving environment as alibis for poor performance.

Certain knowledges, which will be amplified in Chapter 3, are important and helpful to the teacher. These are:

1. Knowledge of good body mechanics in general, in terms of basic alignment and body movement.
2. Knowledge of the basic principles of physics, particularly in relation to springboard use and ballistics.
3. Knowledge of teaching progression in all its ramifications of method, timing, and psychology.
4. Knowledge and awareness of safety factors—not to emphasize danger, but to keep questionable tendencies from becoming hazardous practices.

Patience and flexibility of method should pervade all teaching—the patience to try again and again, and to understand the many possible complications, the flexibility to change a method which does not work, to open the mind to new possibilities of attack.

One last comment: fight your own discouragement. If *you* are at your wits' end, so will the student be. Discouragement is very hard to avoid or to conceal. Diving is a slow-progressing skill to learn; a long, hard, sticky climb. Plateaus are frequent and sometimes permanent. There is no answer except work and ingenuity of new angles and fresh attacks. The diver will get there if you and he keep going. The diver *must* come halfway and do his part. You must inspire him to do so; you must give him the necessary prodding and knowhow. When everything is at a standstill, stop and think: Have I tried all possible approaches? Is the diver working with sincere effort? Have I succeeded in giving him a real understanding of his actions? Try to size up the situation rationally and keep your judgment objective. It is so easy to become the victim of your own desire to have the diver succeed. *Your* frustration, irritation and anger soon transfer to the bewildered diver, who is pleading for help and understanding.

2

General Teaching Techniques

A. DIVING AND AGE GROUPS

1) Children

How old should children be before they are taught to dive? Certainly they must know how to swim to the point of being comfortable and safe in deep water. One sometimes sees a father or mother treading water, begging and cajoling a small child to go off a board, and ready to pull him up and carry him to the side. Such a sight makes any aquatic instructor shudder, both for the safety of the child and for the fright and dislike he may retain for anything to do with water. The parents here are breaking one of the cardinal rules of water safety: *Do not teach diving until you are certain the student can swim safely.*

Even if a child should learn to swim very early, he should not be *taught* diving before he is six, and then only from the side of the pool or perhaps a standing dive from the board. In most cases a six-year-old has not the strength or coordination for the delicate balances of springboard diving, nor does he have the concentration or motivation for the exacting practice.

From ages seven to nine, simple low board (one meter) dives can be taught, and at age ten, high board (three meter) work can be started. There is no hard and fast rule that an eight-year-old could not dive from a high board, any more than there is any guarantee that all ten-year-olds are ready to learn. These are approximate age groupings based on general experience.

In teaching youngsters from six to ten years of age, teaching sessions should be short. The teacher should begin with a few minutes of elementary instruction within a swimming lesson, and develop into perhaps ten or fifteen minutes of diving concentration. By the time they are nine or ten, children should be able to take thirty or forty minutes. The short sessions are advisable because the attention span is short in the young, and the chilling effects of being wet, many times under conditions of wind, cool temperatures, or cloudy skies, is felt much sooner by the little ones.

The best approach to teaching children is through games or stunts involving imagination. From the side of the pool they can be taught the seal dive (p. 40), or the dive from one knee (p. 40), sometimes called the Indian dive. They can dive *for* things on the pool bottom, such as rubber rings, or rounded white stones on a sandy bottom. They enjoy playing follow-the-leader, doing various jumps such as the tuck jump, pike jump, jump half twist, and long jump (see pp. 91–92). A fall-in sit backwards can be tried, or a front jump sit.

Sit-in backward

Front jump-sit

For those working on the springboard, poles can be extended to jump over, dive over, or reach for. Two people holding a rope can set up the same challenges. In using physical devices for training, be prepared to lower them instantly as needed. Avoid frightening those students who have a fear and mistrust of these physical barriers.

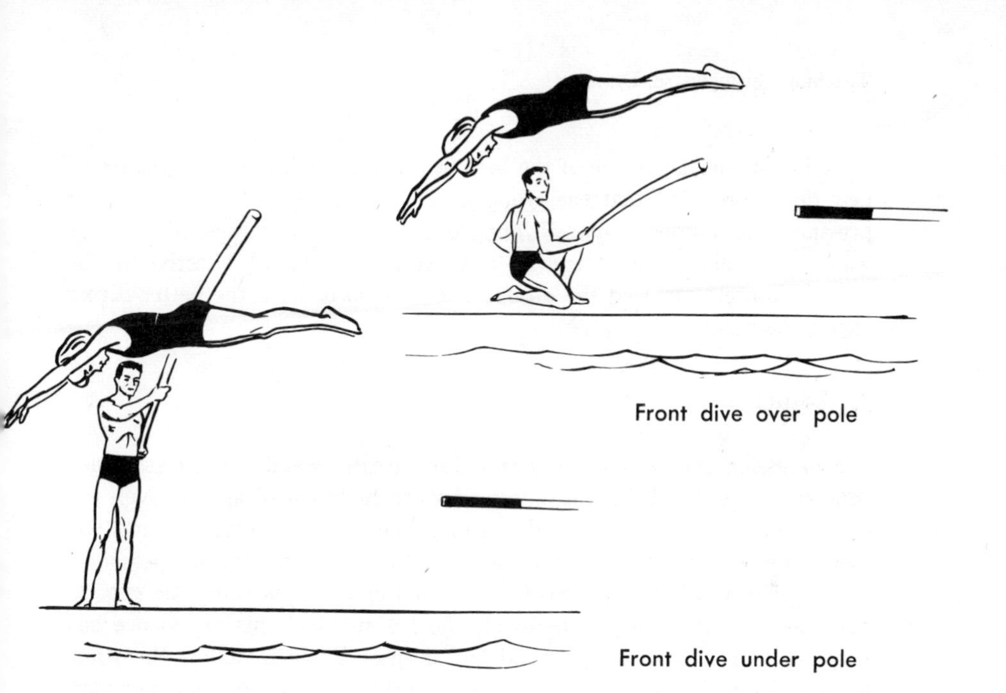

Front dive over pole

Front dive under pole

Front jump, pole overhead

Follow-the-leader is one of the best techniques for introducing phases of new dives, provided that the group as a whole is ready for them. Group pressure will influence many youngsters to try new things which they would not quite dare to try by themselves. It is most effective if the teacher himself can lead the group; next best is to have the better divers take turns leading.

2) Adults

Progression and techniques do not vary greatly whether the class is for children or adults. With beginners who are high school age or over one encounters more inhibition and caution. The tempo of teaching must be much slower and must include more explanation. The mature person is too aware of what will happen if he does not do the right thing: he *expects* the sting of a flat entry. The child who has not had this experience has only positive instructions in mind and is more likely to follow them implicitly. There is a little more chance of accident with the older beginner, since the teacher is never quite sure what effect various preconceived notions and fears will have on the dive action.

The teacher must have the full consent of the adult beginner before trying new dive actions. Nevertheless it is possible to treat an adult group dictatorially from time to time with good results. Sometimes it is effective to declare a "back dive day" or equivalent. The shock treatment of having everyone do some phase of the back dive, whether it has ever been attempted before, is surprisingly successful.

Follow-the-leader, if not over-worked, still has great appeal even for college-age students. A game suitable for intermediate and advanced divers is "calling" dives. The diver begins his approach, not knowing what dive he is to do. At the third step, going into the hurdle, the instructor calls out a specific dive. The challenge is to be able to think quickly and keep one's balance to execute whatever is called. It might be a plain front dive, a somersault, a twist, or even a front jump. Back takeoff dives are left out, of course, and it is not advisable to include any from the reverse group. The instructor must choose dives or skills which he knows that diver has mastered. This is a game for practice in learned skills, not for trying out new ones.

B. GROUP TEACHING TECHNIQUES

Diving is fundamentally an individual activity, of necessity taught in groups varying in size from eight to thirty students. In an ideal group of about six divers one can combine good teaching and personal coaching. Everyone gets a chance to dive frequently without getting chilled in between, and yet there is enough interval to be able to think over and absorb coaching points. One or two divers is too small a group: the individuals get too tired, the tempo is too fast to get the most out of instruction, and there is not enough opportunity for them to profit from seeing others' faults and improvements.

What are the problems of the large class, which is the most common situation at camps, Y's, schools, clubs, and colleges? The teacher sees too many too fast. It is impossible to give a great deal of individual help if the class is larger than ten students. The teacher is harrassed by questions and "watch me's" simultaneously. He is frustrated trying to remember coaching points for individuals after seeing many divers in a row. Meanwhile the class members stand and freeze, or become discipline problems. Accident possibilities tend to increase as the number in the class is increased and the teacher is more distracted.

There are compromises which ease the situation. You can give instructions to the group as a whole on skills which everyone should be able to manage safely. Keep the entire group momentarily at that level since perhaps you do not yet know which ones are your dangerous beginners. Sort out those behind and ahead of the group and begin to organize them as separate groups, giving them instruction specific to their needs. Eventually allow individuals to work on their own level within the total group. As much as possible try to *group* those who are at the same level.

Within any class of students there are many levels of skill. Those who have learned some dives already may be ahead of the beginners in most ways. Yet, having learned these dives under another instructor (or on their own), the problem of conflicting methods and styles is possible. Every teacher has his particular pet ideas. To change teachers is not an easy adjustment for the diver. The conflict of method and loyalty may upset his diving disastrously. When faced with the problem of teaching a diver who has learned many skills elsewhere, one must go slowly and with diplomacy. It is often best to let him continue a style or technique with which you do not agree, unless that technique is of great detriment to his progress.

The self-made diver poses some of the same problems. He will take pride in all that he has done on his own and may be stubborn when it comes to correcting faults which he cherishes as accomplishments.

The joy of any class is the student who starts from the beginning with you, shows promise from the first day, and continues to learn well and quickly. You realize that you have someone with the physical potential and skill to go far in diving. This student is exciting to teach, tempting to lead on fast, but remember that there is great responsibility involved. Of all your students this one must be taught most carefully. Where in general group teaching you may be forced into superficial correction, with this student you must be more severe, more demanding, and more detailed in coaching. If the student is aware of his potential and is genuinely interested, he will appreciate your concern and will work very hard.

In the large group, follow the procedure of teaching every dive from the beginning for everyone. By this method initial instructions can be given for everyone at the same time. The advanced divers may complain, but getting back to the beginning is good review for everyone, and often is the only way to detect and correct basic faults which are causing troubles in the finished dive. For each dive the class will soon divide itself into those who can and those who cannot. Here is a sample lesson plan for a large group starting on a front jackknife:

1) Warm up with front dives. Teacher take note of those whose takeoffs are poor.
2) Sort out the few you consider not yet ready to try the jackknife. Tell these to keep working on the front dive, giving them a few tips.
3) Have other class members stand aside while poor ones continue to practice.
4) Give other class members initial instructions for the front jackknife.
5) Everyone back to the board for first tries. Let them try two or three apiece.
6) Weed out the better ones; leave the rest to practice.
7) Give the better ones more advanced coaching points.
8) Back to the board for all; practice.
9) Give the poor ones, still on the front dive, special attention. If any or all are ready, give them front jack knife instructions.
10) On the board for all. Individual coaching as time permits.

3

Principles of Movement in Diving

A. UNDERLYING PHYSICAL PRINCIPLES

There are basic principles of body movement which should be understood before teaching diving. These principles should not only be understood initially by the teacher but should be kept in mind and reviewed frequently. They should be taught to the students directly or indirectly as suits the occasion.

The laws of physics relating to mechanics are the laws of diving. All the things that we know to govern the behavior of inanimate objects at rest and in motion also govern the behavior of the human diver.

1. STANCE

To bring the physics of diving closer to the teaching of diving we will consider practical aspects which should help in teaching and correcting. First look at the student as he stands. He maintains balance (equilibrium) by keeping the center of the mass (usually called the center of gravity) over the base of support. Is the student aligned correctly as he stands normally? This means a vertical alignment of the weight-bearing segments through the center of gravity of the body, each segment thus providing a firm base of support for the segment above. In visual checking from the side, the ear, back of the neck at the top of the shoulders, center of the hip joint, knee and ankle joints should all be in line. If this basic standing position is out of line in respect to these joints, whether due to bad habit, ignorance, lack of muscle tone, or faulty bone structure, the imbalances resulting will tend to exist to some degree when the body is in motion.

The nature of diving is such that a force is given to the body, partly from the muscle action of the body spring and partly from the energy released by the deflected board as it snaps back to a straight position. This energy is most efficiently used if it can generate force in line with the body segments. The result of the force (in diving—height) is far greater from a spring through a body in good alignment than through a body out of alignment. A flexible body out of alignment is not in the best position to utilize effectively the energy from the board. It may absorb within itself a part of this energy.

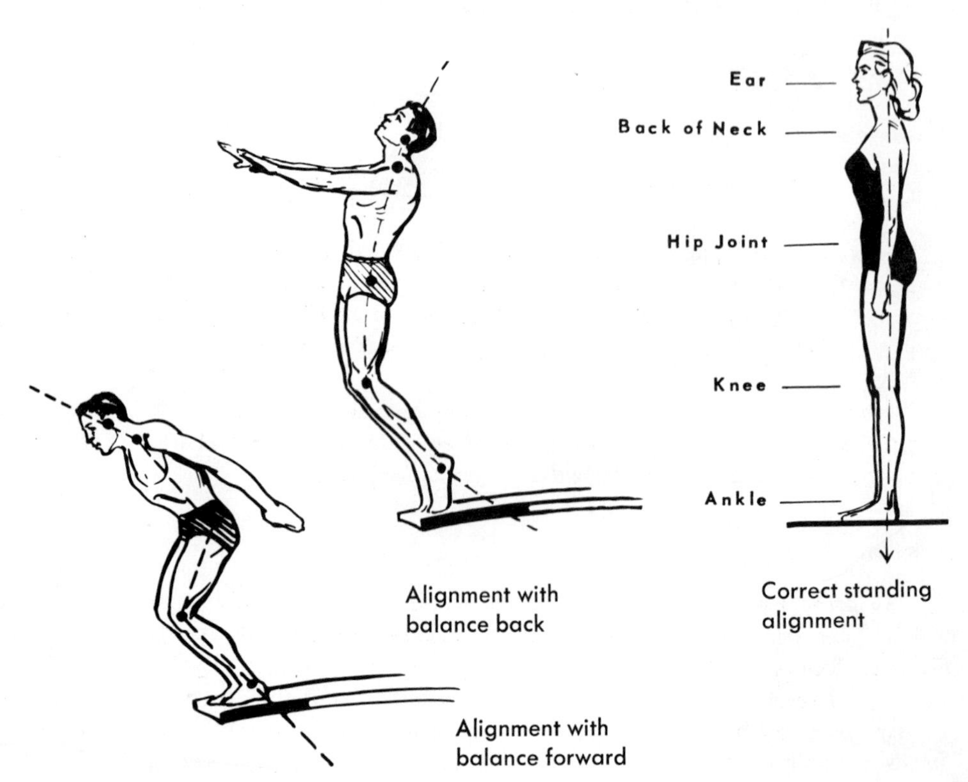

Alignment with balance back

Correct standing alignment

Alignment with balance forward

2. STEPS

As the diver stands in readiness for a forward approach, his balance should be a delicate one. The body should be in alignment, but there should be a slightly forward imbalance to allow an easy, quick transfer into forward motion. Weight absolutely centered or a degree toward the heels means that the inertia will be more difficult to overcome when the steps begin.

As the diver starts his walk, check his mechanics for smooth and even application of force through the feet, and for functional movement without unnecessary and over-compensated instabilities. Although the total body line must tilt forward in order to move in that direction, he should maintain good alignment and lean forward only as far as is needed for the speed of the walk.

3. HURDLE

The object of what is done on the board is to achieve an arc of maximum height in the air by utilizing the spring of the board. As a projectile, the diver's body will rise from the board in height proportional to the downward force applied against the board. In order to achieve height in the air the diver must drop to the tip of the board from a high and effective leap. This is known as the hurdle.

The hurdle converts muscular energy into height. As the diver falls from this height, this energy is next converted into energy of motion, which, upon impact with the board, is again converted into elastic energy in the deflected board. Upon impact the diver furthermore crouches, which does two things: a) it provides a longer, smoother, more efficient transfer to the board of his energy of motion, and b) it cocks his muscular mechanism for a second release of muscular energy. As the board reaches its maximum downward position, it springs an elastic release of its energy (equal to that of the hurdle) to project the diver upward (every action has an opposite and equal reaction). Now the diver adds a second release of muscular energy to that of the stored first release, and the resulting projection is twice as powerful as either alone. This accumulation of energy could be continued indefinitely (by bouncing the board), except that the diver isn't stopping to do this, but is on his way into the water.

How much one can achieve in a single hurdle will depend on the weight of the diver, the muscle strength he has to apply force, and the timing of the application of this force in relation to the spring or elasticity of the board. Therefore the position and balance of the body as it falls to the board tip are of utmost importance—and the position and balance are direct outcomes of the hurdle. The hurdle encompasses movement from the beginning of the third step (in a three-step approach) to the point of contact with the toes on the board tip. A forceful push into the hurdle is started by increasing the normal knee flexion of the weight-bearing leg, thus lowering the body's weight. Subsequently this leg is strongly extended along with an upward reach of the arms. The drop from the peak of the hurdle lift is accompanied by gravitational pull. There is a release of strong muscular tension, yet enough tension remains to control balance. The body must be in its best vertical alignment just as the board tip is reached, but also in an equilibrium delicate enough to adjust quickly as the board bends and directs the body slightly forward and up. The diver will throw away potential height if he lands on the tip off balance. He will also throw it away if he fails to complete his takeoff push. Once he has left the board his flight is set and he cannot change it. This basic premise means that good divers usually know at this point whether or not the dive will be good.

4. POINT OF TAKEOFF

Without forward motion the body will be projected vertically upward and will subsequently return vertically downward to the exact point of departure. This is what one does when bouncing. A forward velocity, when added to the vertical projection, results in a takeoff path tilted forward from the vertical. The diver adds just enough forward velocity to make an arc which will pass the board tip with proper clearance for safety.

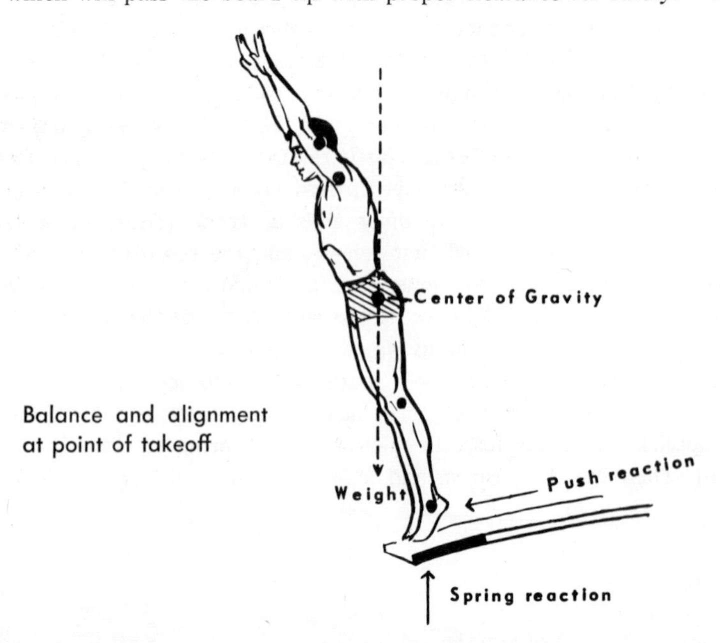

Balance and alignment
at point of takeoff

This clearance must also be achieved for standing dives which have no forward velocity. It is achieved by a slight forward lean and a slight push back from the feet. The board's reaction would be a forward thrust on the feet. The vertical reaction of the board passes behind the center of gravity causing a forward rotation. Adding the horizontal reaction to the foot thrust causes a backward rotation, which can be controlled according to what is desired for the dive. Since standing dives on the springboard are almost always those in the backward and inward groups, consider the application of these statements as a backward lean and a slight push forward from the feet.

The diver may easily control his rotation by applying a slightly larger or smaller horizontal push. (Likewise at the start of the forward walk, the same actions occur, but without the vertical force. The backward push and the forward lean permit a horizontal acceleration of the center of gravity without toppling backwards or pitching forward.)

5. FLIGHT

On the rise from the board there will be a deceleration of velocity until the point of greatest height is reached. The diver can sense this stopping point before descent of the body toward the water begins. On the way down there is acceleration in velocity of the falling body. The diver is making an arc (parabola) and at the same time accomplishing a rotation around his own center of gravity. A plain front dive, for example, is a half rotation, having started with the diver on his feet and ending head first. Rotary movement is not present in simple jumps, but is present in every other dive in a forward or backward direction.

After takeoff the problem is one of controlling body position according to the requirements of that particular dive. The diver utilizes the force of his own takeoff and the board's elasticity to initiate his mechanics of execution in the air. From the peak of height downward he concentrates on controlling his position for proper entry. The only specific areas under his control at any time are a) his own *body position* within the arc set at the takeoff and b) the *rate of rotation* around his own center.

a) *Body Position* The diver can assume and change his position in the air by muscular action during the flight by moving his head, holding or moving his arms, flexing his hips or knees, flexing or extending the spine. The positions or position changes along the path of the flight comprise the traditional dives we know and recognize.

b) *Rate of Rotation* The diver can influence the rate of his rotation within the flight, set at point of takeoff both by the position he assumes and by the manner in which he assumes this position. A rotating body has two factors which affect its rate of rotation: the masses of the body, and the positioning of these masses. Once the rotation has been initiated, its energy is established and cannot be changed in the air.

Consider two configurations of a pair of equally balanced balls in rotation. The individual balls try to move in a straight path (dotted) but the tension in the bar holding them keeps pulling them inward, thus causing motion in a circular path. One can see that the degree of curvature of these two paths is quite different. Now the energy of each system is a matter of the mass of the balls, the speed of the balls along their individual paths, and the radius from the ball to the pivot. If each arrangement has the same total energy, the one with the smaller radius will have to have a greater speed to compensate for its more compact arrangement. This will result in a much faster rate of rotation.

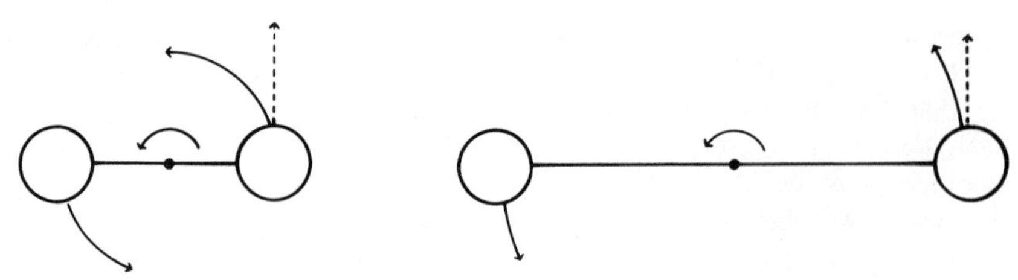

Balls with short radius

Balls with long radius

This is how the diver can speed up or slow down a rotation without recourse to an external reaction. The rotation must have been initiated by an external reaction (the board), but once established, it is there. All that can be done about it is to control and modify its rate and the duration of any selected rate. The duration, in turn, can control the amount of rotation occurring between the starting and stopping of any particular phase of a dive. Study the differences in rotation between a swan dive and a double somersault in tuck position (rolled up like a ball). The swan dive is a stretched-out position, the extremities being at their maximum distance from the center of rotation in the hips. Thus the speed of rotation will be slow, which is desirable in only a half turn of the body. A double somersault in tuck position folds the body close together, bringing the extremities closer to the center for faster turning.

Rate of rotation in spins will also be influenced by three other factors:

1) *Method of assuming the position* The direction and the degree of rotation are set by the takeoff push, but the diver has some muscular control over the manner in which he assumes the position for spinning. For example, in a forward somersault tuck, he may only half tuck, slowing his rotation. Or he may lift his knees too hard toward his hands without the correct downward throw of the arms. His proper control is a forceful downward throw of the head and arms while at the same time the lower body folds in the hands. Because the body as a whole is rotating from the board, the lower body appears to fold back and up.

2) *Timing of assuming the position* The movement into the desired body position must be started very soon after takeoff, making fullest use of the rotational force achieved at takeoff. The coaches' maxim is to spin "on the way up."

3) *Angle of takeoff* The more forward the angle of takeoff is, the faster will be the spin. This is not always desirable in literal application, or divers would sacrifice height. Taken as a very few degrees one way or another, it is true that the more turns to be done, the greater should be the lean forward on the takeoff.

6. ENTRY

a) *Body position* Entries are either head first or foot first, and basic vertical alignment is again important in maintaining a streamlined position for minimizing splash and carrying the body to the bottom. Since head-first entries are predominant, it would be well to check the student's basic alignment upside down in a handstand against a wall, a handstand in shallow water, or in the finishing position of a surface dive.

b) *Entry "spot"* At the point of entry the diver must enter the water a few degrees short of the vertical, since his body rotation will tend to continue into the water. Control so that the falling body does not rotate beyond the desired attitude on entry is a matter of muscular tension plus visual aim. On the downward flight it is essential to aim for an imaginary spot on the surface of the water. To the diver this entry point must appear to be six to twelve inches farther from the board than he would consider exactly vertical (as seen from the top of the dive).

c) *Rotation* A diver upon entering the water will feel water resistance against his arms and shoulders, and will have to fight the tendency for his legs to go over. This sequence of events occurs because all dives enter the water with some rotation about the diver's center of gravity. As the hands contact the water, the rotational motion they have meets the reaction of the water, producing a reduced rotation and a forward motion of the center of gravity itself. In other words, the hands become fixed and become the pivot. The legs keep on moving forward (in the direction of the original rotation). Properly executed, the body will rotate to the vertical as it enters the water.

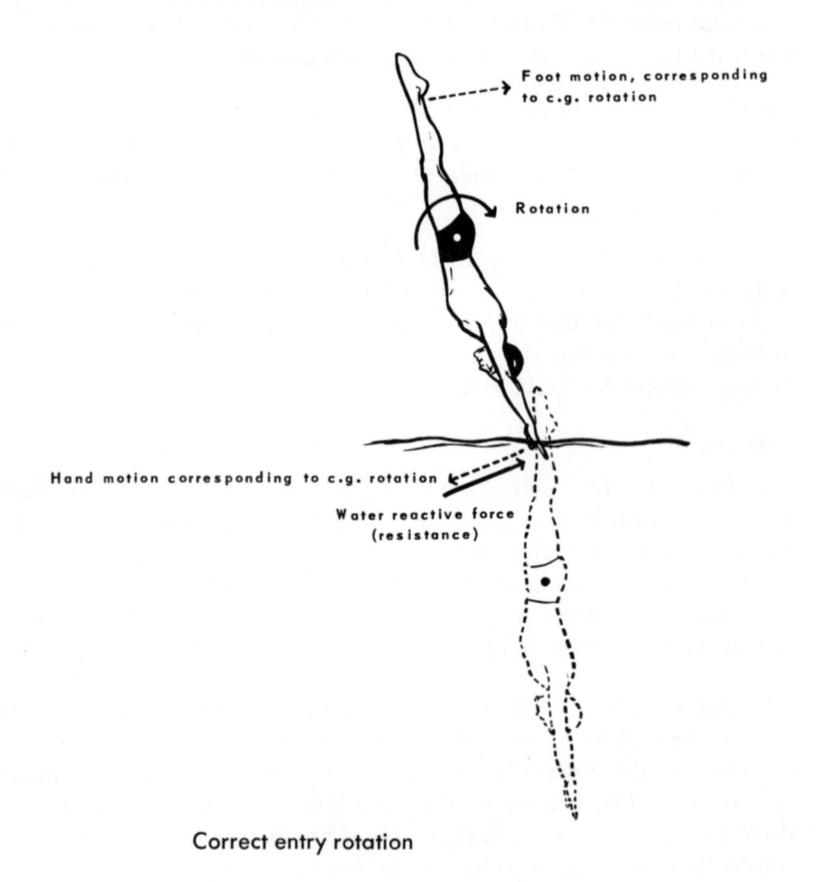

Correct entry rotation

A forward dive which is vertical or beyond vertical at contact will cartwheel over the hands to land on its back. Even if the diver attempts to counteract his going over by pulling up underwater, his back will arch considerably and his knees will tend to collapse.

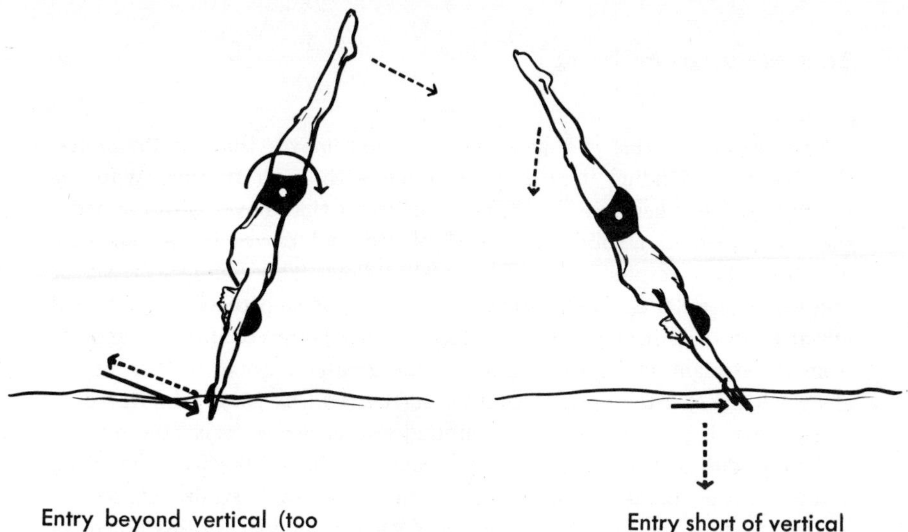

Entry beyond vertical (too much rotation)

Entry short of vertical (insufficient rotation)

A forward dive which is lacking in rotational rate and is heading into the water at too flat an angle will tend to drop even flatter after the hands contact.

d) *Underwater path* From the point of contact of the fingertips or toes with the water, the diver falls on a slight curve following hands or toes into the same hole. The body must be extended as it passes through the water until bottom is reached, or at least until momentum is substantially decelerated by water resistance. If this extension during the fall into and through the water is not held, the tunnel actually made in the water by the diver will be disturbed. Splash will be increased even on what appeared at the surface to be a straight entry.

Path of good entry

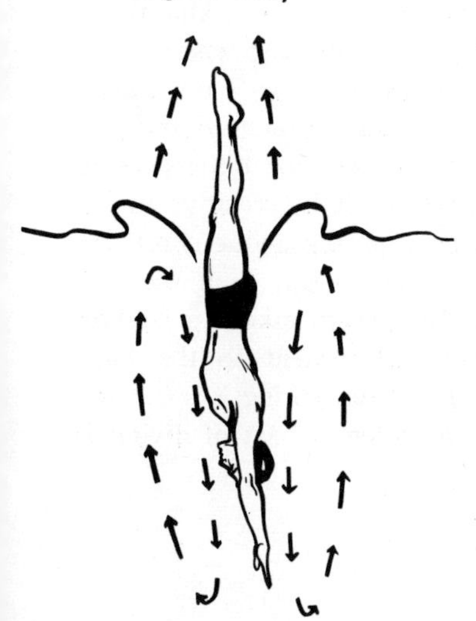

Path of bad entry

The reason for this is that when an object moves through the water, the water surrounding it is dragged along with it by friction. Water is incompressible. Therefore, for every bit of water that moves with the body, there is an equal amount that is displaced and moves in the opposite direction. This results in two currents of flow. The counter-current or upward flow wells up at the surface but does not stop there. It continues upward resulting in a geyser or splash. If the body collapses or departs from its straight and narrow path, a far greater current will be drawn along with it and the upward counter-current will be greatly increased.

An early break in body position underwater while it is still moving fast may, due to its downward force, cause strains at the joints involved in the position break. These might be neck and back strains caused by lifting the head or arms too soon, or perhaps shoulder strains when an arm is wide on a head first entry.

B. KINESTHETIC AWARENESS

The positions of the various body segments are controlled by muscles, which are in turn affected by the nervous system. The body movement is thus accomplished by conscious muscle work. The work resulting is affected by related sensations from the balance center of the ear; proprioceptors in the muscles, tendons, and joints; by the judgment of the eye in terms of distance and depth; and by the "mind's eye"—the awareness of what is being achieved, or, in a sense, by what one *thinks* one looks like. Everyone of these aspects has its part in successful movement. It is a delicate adjustment of physical and mental impressions and expressions into tangible visible performance.

Certainly diving is an activity of fine neuromuscular control. The most essential part of the neuromuscular system to the diver is kinesthetic awareness. The diver must know where he is in space, and where every part of himself is in relation to his moving center. He must have a good kinesthetic "feel" for the slightest variation in his relation to the pull of gravity, for speed of motion, for rate of rotation, for differences in board flexibilities and how this affects him. He must be sensitive to the movement which comes with ease and the one requiring undue effort. He must be as at home upside down as he is rightside up. In a way, no matter how expert and consistent a diver becomes, every takeoff is slightly different. Every dive is thus an on-the-spot adjustment to the force and height and rotation as produced by that particular spring.

The kinesthetic awareness which is such an integral part of diving is closely related to and influenced by the use of the eyes. One's feeling of position in space comes a good deal from the visual relating of objects. From the beginning fall-ins, students should consciously use their eyes to focus on definite points of aim. The fact that the eyes are open is not enough—in fact, to see the walls or clouds or people or water swing by with no focus is most confusing. Definite spots or points should be used as points of aim and judgment.

C. TEACHING PRINCIPLES OF MOVEMENT

The principles discussed concerning the physical mechanics of diving, along with the all-pervading influence of kinesthetic awareness, must be *taught*. Divers must be keenly conscious of them if they are to improve, and conscious to some degree from the very beginning. A continuous process of self-evaluation best helps the individual diver. As a point of re-emphasis, don't *tell* them what happened that was wrong: ask them what did they *feel*. Make them conscious of every movement they make and of the result therefrom. The first dives, and all new dives, are almost always a matter of luck—an obedient action with no sensation except blankness or dizziness or surprise. It is not until the movement is willed and consciously performed that it becomes comfortable, graceful, and can be called forth at will.

D. GENERAL AND PARTICULAR STRENGTHS AND FLEXIBILITIES

1. STRENGTH

A diver need not have great strength. A sense of timing in spring, good alignment control, good sense of balance, and generally healthy muscle condition will suffice. True, certain areas of strength develop through diving, and work in these areas often improves diving. The number one area of strength needed is abdominal. These muscles initiate much of forward motion, forward spins, and work very hard in controlling and stopping body rotation at the entry point, even continuing to work under water. Vertical alignment to start with involves abdominal control. The extensor muscles of the back also play a strong role in entry control, balancing the abdominal contraction. More entries are forward than backward, so perhaps the abdominals actually have more work to do.

Head first, forward

Head first, backward

Foot first, forward

Foot first, backward

AREAS OF MUSCLE CONTROL ON ENTRIES

In addition to these two muscle areas, the leg extensors are important to spring into the dive and to hold alignment. The leg flexors work in the direction of the pull of gravity, so they have an easy time of it. Body extension is aided by hip extensors (buttocks), knee extensors (thighs and calves), ankle extensors, and toe flexors. The strength of the feet in extension is very important as the feet are the terminal point of contact and drive from the board.

Many muscles in the body, if not all, participate in the process of diving due to the rotation of the body with all its changing relationships to the pull of gravity. A good deal of this general muscle action is of a stabilizing nature, a holding of position.

One muscle area perhaps not directly concerned with the dive becomes much stronger: that is the triceps (the extensors of the elbow). This muscle is constantly at work as the diver lands on the bottom to keep him from crashing into it. It also develops because many divers hoist themselves directly over the edge of the pool side instead of using ladders. The ladder, in turn, will develop his biceps.

2. FLEXIBILITY

Areas of flexibility do not have to be great, but are important to a degree in terms of ankle flexion and extension, and normal range of movement in back and shoulders. Angle flexion, a stretching of the heel cord, increases the range of movement in the total leg spring. Angle extension, or what we think of as a good pointed toe, is necessary for completion of spring and for correct form throughout the rest of the dive. Hip flexion, a stretching of the hamstrings, makes the pike position easier and spins faster. Back flexibility, the ability to "arch," has great drawbacks if overdone. Undue use of back flexibility in extension will cut off height, cause undesired sags in form dives such as the swan dive or half twist, and will prevent the diver from entering the water in proper alignment. Shoulder flexibility, particularly in retraction, allows the arms to line up directly with the sides of the head for good entries.

4

Exercises for Diving

Here is a suggested list of exercises for strength and flexibility particularly related to diving. Courses of general conditioning help greatly and frequently will reach the same areas of weakness. These below have been selected from practical experience to work into a diving instruction program.

A. GOOD FOR ALL LEVELS OF DIVING

1) Back lying, arms stretched overhead, knees bent, feet on floor. Flatten back to floor and relax. Repeat with straighter knees until exercise can be done with legs straight (maintaining arm stretch overhead).

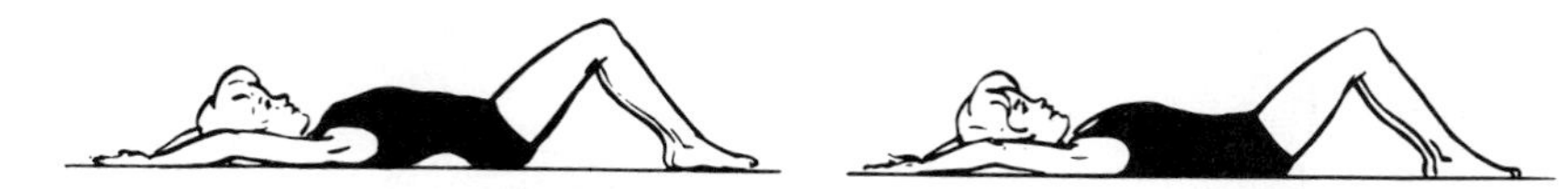

2) Long sitting position. Roll back to flat back position, arms overhead.

3) Face lying, arms to side. Lift as in swan dive, from hips and from shoulders, with stress on thoracic rather than lumbar extension.

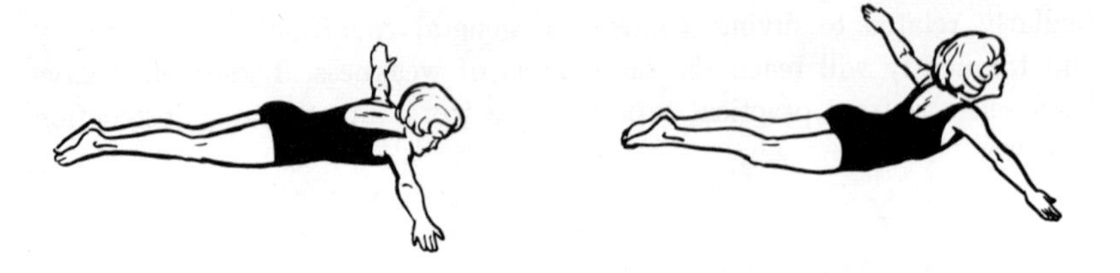

4) Stand facing stall bar or ledge at least waist high, one leg on bar. Bend forward over raised leg, both legs straight.

5) Standard push-ups.

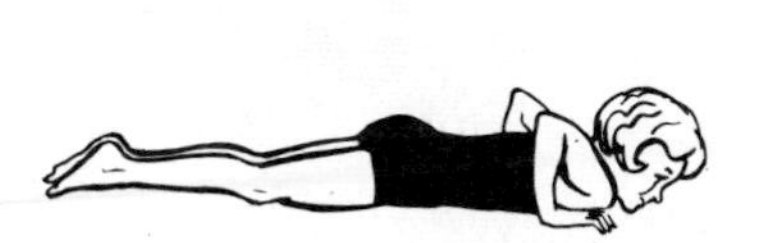

6) Stand about one foot from wall. Arms forward, lean into wall with body straight and heels on floor. Increase distance from wall as heel cord stretches.

7) Standing in good alignment, one hand on bar or wall for balance, one arm overhead. Controlled slow rising on toes and return (relever). Work with both arms overhead eventually, and one foot at a time. Maintain body alignment.

8) Standing position. Step, lift arms and knee into hurdle position with relever on straight leg. Return bent leg to position one step behind. Repeat (see pp. 71–72).

9) Slow walk lifting alternate knees into hurdle position with strong ankle extension on both legs.

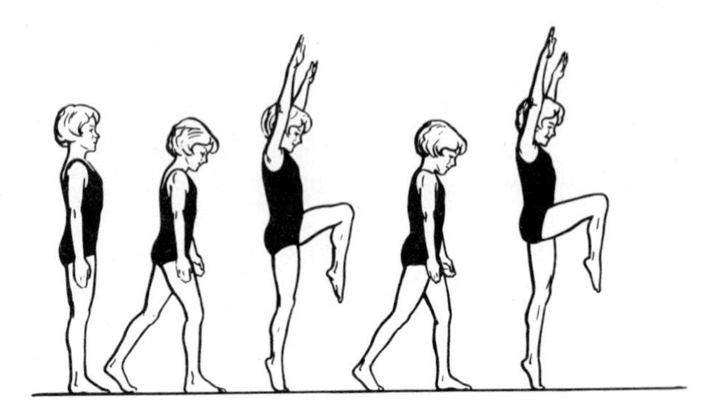

10) Same with more speed, making it a continuous run ("pedalling").
11) Standard back takeoff swings with progressive jumps backward (about 6 inches); (see p. 86).

12) Light jumping in place, working from relevers into elevation. Stress ankle and knee flexion and extension, not elevation.

B. FOR INTERMEDIATE AND ADVANCED DIVERS

13) Situps from floor and from an inclined board with head low.

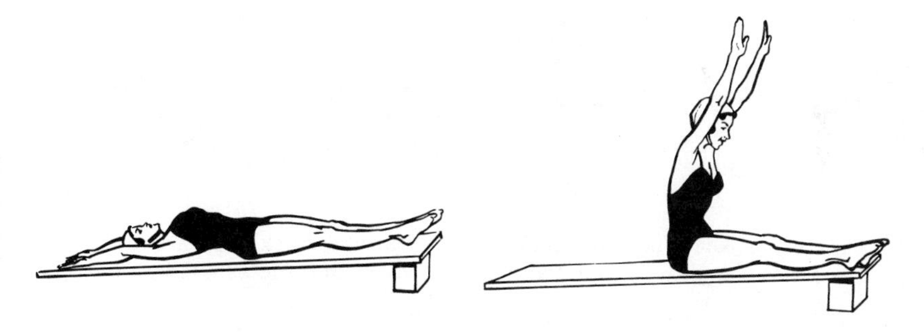

14) Hang from horizontal bar. Do repeated leg lifts as high as possible.

15) Back lying, open pike position with legs perpendicular. Pull legs back into tighter pike position and return. Keep head, shoulders, and arms in contact with floor.

16) Back lying, tuck position with feet off floor. Stretch legs to pike position, flexing ankles; extend ankles and return.

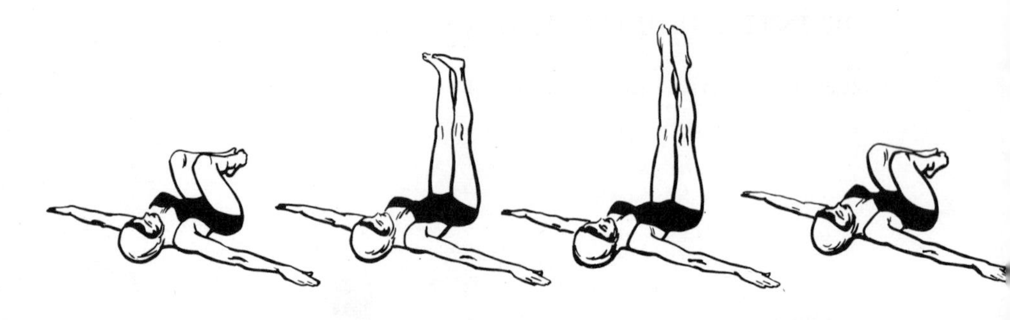

17) Hands-knees position, back flat, head in line. Tuck one knee as far as possible, then extend the same leg back and alternate arm forward, keeping back flat.

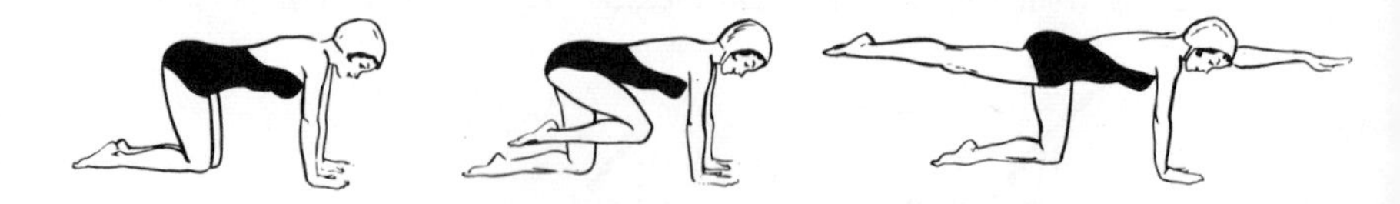

18) Kneel on towel with toes extended. Sit back on ankles and rock, slightly supporting body weight with hands placed on floor beside legs. Knees lift off the floor.

19) High skips in hurdle position, emphasizing push of feet, height from floor and body position.

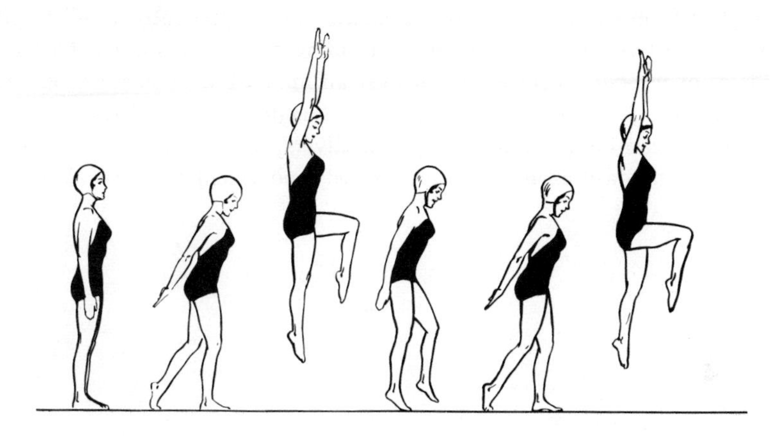

20) Stand about three feet from a block or step. Take a one-step hurdle toward the step, landing on it with two feet. Try to keep pushing leg straight after press (see p. 73).

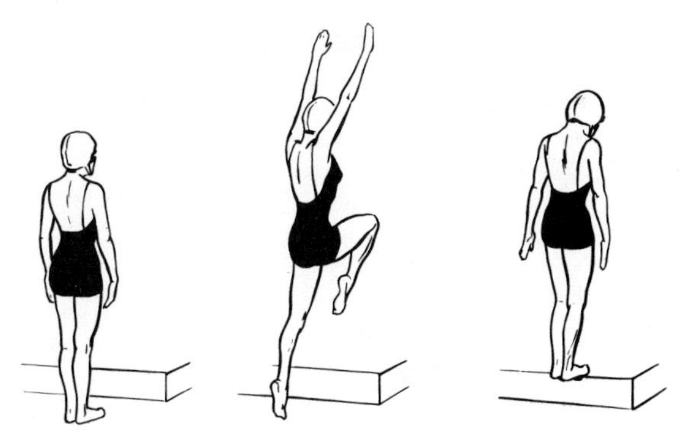

21) Handstands against wall, about one foot from wall. Alternately arch and flatten back.

ISOMETRIC CONTRACTION

The form of strength training called "isometric contraction" is producing effective results currently in training for many sports. This is a process of muscular contraction against an immovable resistance, building strength of specific muscle groups but not endurance. I believe this type of exercise can be of value for training divers, but I have had experience only with standard exercises involving body movement as listed above.

5

Equipment

Equipment for diving is very simple: a board from which to dive, and a body of water into which to dive. Specifications for this simple equipment, however, are quite exacting.

What is a diving board? A diving board is a plank extending over water. It can be made of one piece of wood, or several pieces of wood laminated (glued together), or of wood with a fiberglass coating, or of metal—most often aluminum.

The main points are that it is fixed at one end, has a fulcrum on which it rests one third to one half the way out, is long enough to take at least three steps comfortably, has a slight degree of slope upward, is not so narrow as to give a diver that tightrope feeling, and is springy.

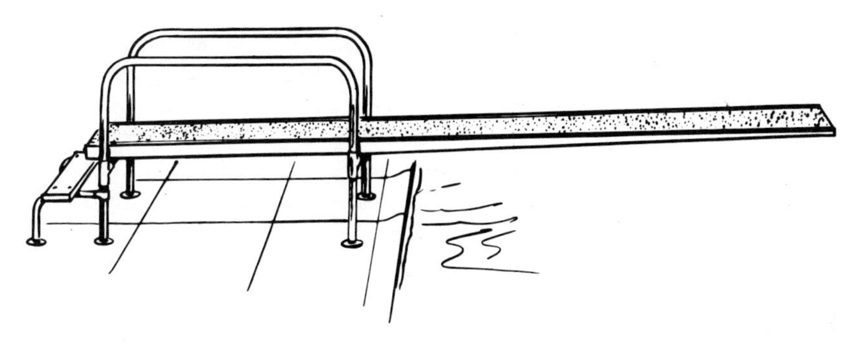

More technically, boards should be twenty inches wide, fourteen to sixteen feet long, tapered from three inches thickness at the fixed end to one and a half inches at the free end. The board should have a slight uphill pitch of not more than two inches from the fixed end to the tip. The surface should be non-slippery—the most satisfactory kind has a glued-on sandpaper sort of finish (bare wood is lethal; sand-in-paint doesn't last; heavy canvas is fine at first, but becomes slick in a very short time; rubber matting and cocoa matting are fair, but seal in moisture next to wood and can cause rotting).

Many times it is not practical or necessary to meet all the specifications of the competitive board as described above. Perhaps you have a backyard pool for children; are in a camp situation or a pool where perfect installation is impossible; or are limited by finances. A board can be twelve feet long or even slightly shorter for children; it can be home-made of seasoned wood, preferably Douglas Fir or Oregon Pine. For safety and use in developing good diving, follow the general specifications above for length, width, fulcrum placement, pitch, and surface.[1]

There is no reason that boards of non-official height from the water cannot be used, and used to great advantage. One meter and three meters from the water are the two heights of springboards used in all competition (called "low" and "high"). Nevertheless the one-foot or two-foot board has great challenge and learning value. Five-, six-, or seven-foot boards are excellent for progressive stages in working up to the ten-foot board (three meters). The only drawback of the unorthodox heights is in the *sole* use of these boards by a diver who is actively engaged in one or three meter competition.

The FULCRUM is the horizontal bar upon which the board rests, and is the part at which there is maximum stress. This is covered with a sound-and-shock-absorbing material: live rubber, foam rubber, even old carpeting. Fulcrum placing in relation to the length of the board is a delicate matter, depending on the basic flexibility of the board, the general age and weight of the individuals using the board, and the whims of the advanced competitive diver. Some like boards loose and slow, others stiff and fast, with all the variations in between. These preferences stem somewhat from the weight of the diver, his strength, his body build, and perhaps from the basic rhythmic preference of the individual. Important points about all fulcrums are that they should be installed truly square (at right angles to the long axis of the board), and level, and that they

---

[1] Sydney C. Hazelton and Clifford A. Pulis, *Diving Manual For Instructors* (Hanover, N. H., Fourth Edition, 1956).

should be firmly anchored. A slightly tilted or loose fulcrum may cause a torque in the board as it is sprung, not only sending the diver to one side, but eventually damaging the board. Ideally, fulcrums are movable by a wheel, so that the board can be adapted quickly to individual weight and preference, and the stress on the board itself can be constantly shifted. If the fulcrum is fixed, it should be in such a way that it can be easily adjusted with a few tools, not entirely to cater to the diver, but partly to make adjustments in spring as the board itself changes in flexibility.

In addition to a correctly installed board, the other big essential is WATER. Sounds elementary, but these are the considerations: walls and other boards not too close by, water which is deep enough, and a safe bottom on which to land.

1) Walls and Clearance

Side walls should be at least seven feet away from a one meter board and ten feet from a three meter board. End walls should not be less than five feet back from the board. These distances are obviously for safety, partly to cope with the varying entry directions normally, and partly to safeguard those who bounce out of control. A third justification could be called psychological: a physical barrier such as a wall appears closer to the diver than it is in reality, even though it might be impossible to hit. This is inhibiting.

The boards, if more than one, should not be too close together. Follow the same distance recommendations as for the side walls, allowing a little more space when boards of different heights are involved. There should be free space of twelve feet beyond the tip of the low board, twenty-two feet in front of a high board, and twelve feet above all boards.

2) Depth

Competitive recommendations are ten feet in depth of water for a one meter board and twelve feet for a three meter board. Nine feet is *possible* for the low board and ten feet for the high. Less than this is definitely unsafe. A good entry is close to vertical, and is extremely fast. With arms overhead the diver needs approximately four feet more than his height in order not to hit bottom harder than he can hold. He can "break" his dive position early (just under the surface of the water), but this is detrimental to his entry and to his back. Although a diver can be trained to dive safely in shallow water—*trained* to, not expected to—he should not have to face this hazard.

3) Bottom

The surface of the bottom should be firm and not slippery. Tile is the best, but can vary: small tile is excellent, but wide tile can be very slick. Cement is all right, providing it is neither too smooth nor too rough. Natural bottom—sand, mud, stones—can be satisfactory, but on the whole, depths for diving should exceed specification if the bottom surface is at all questionable. All this is because to dive correctly, the diver should hold his position until he has "hit" bottom; any other procedure in an entry is risky, jeopardizing the entry and the diver's joints. Some highly skilled divers are trained to make quick position changes just under the surface of the water in order to make spectacularly clean entries, but this is for the experts. The "hit" is a landing on the palms of the hands, controlling the falling weight with arm and back muscles, giving with it as one does with the legs and body when landing from a height.

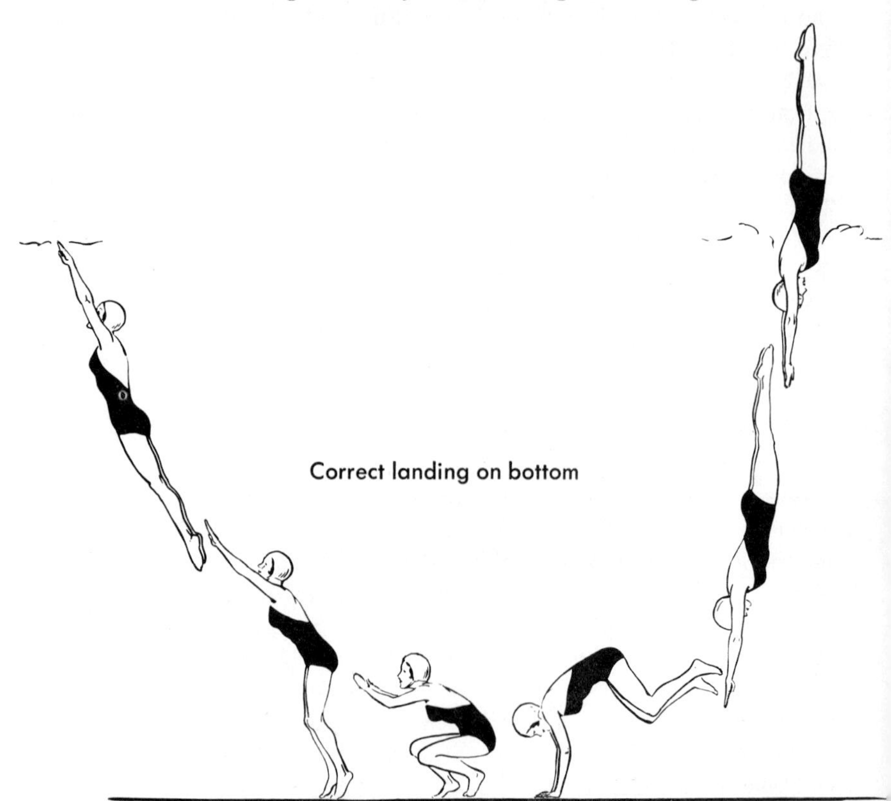

Correct landing on bottom

The only exception to the hitting bottom rule is in the case where there is great depth, and the diver rides straight down until he feels his momentum lessen. In a normal situation, the better the diver, the harder he hits: his angle is nearer to vertical and his body position is streamlined. Therefore he falls less distance through the water and gets there faster.

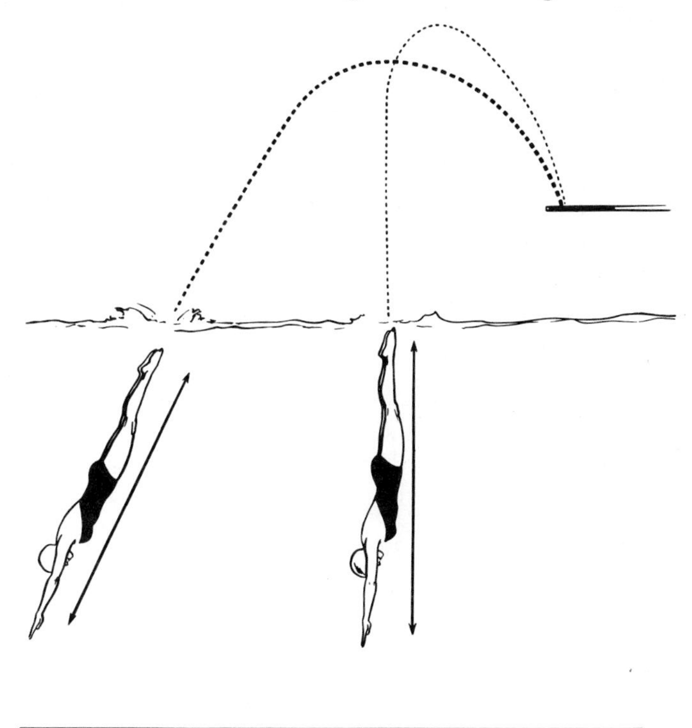

Comparative distance from surface to bottom in correct and far out entry

One last consideration regarding the bottom is its shape. Most dives have directions of rotation which vary the landing point. In these cases the entry is not a drop into the water so that the diver hits bottom directly below his point of entry, but is rather an arc carrying the diver slightly under or away from the board. Also in the learning process of all dives, the entries may cover quite an area. So the bottom should be deep enough over a large area—technically, over the same area as recommended for board clearance (see p. 35). Pools built with so-called "spoon" bottoms or with five foot depths all around the edges so that people can rest there, are problems for divers, often dangerous problems. The ideal is a bottom which is the specified diving depth from the back wall to at least eight feet beyond the board tip.

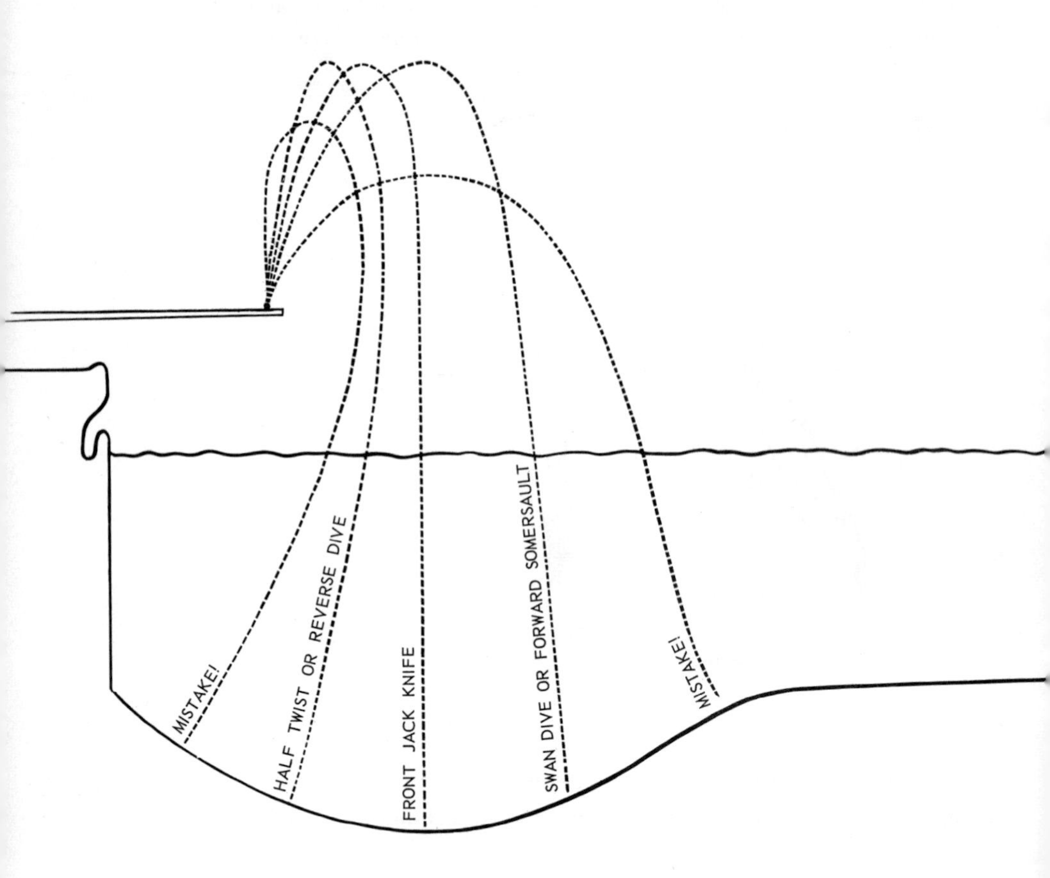

"Spoon bottom" dangers: problems and possibilities

Drains directly below the entry point for dives should be eliminated. These drains should be placed in pairs several feet apart in the center, or back at the end wall. If the drain *must* be under the board, it should be covered with a surface which has no sharp edges and which will not allow fingers or toes to slip through.

6

Before the Board

The basic dive into the water is for the purpose of getting in to swim. So in the beginning we are concerned only with "getting in head first" as easily and smoothly as possible. Yet from the start we can and should teach safety, efficiency, and certain points of indoctrination in spring and entry which are more related to springboard diving. Almost without exception the teaching procedure followed is a step by step progression from a position very close to the water. The standard positions are shown on p. 40.[2]

Individual teachers often have variations of their own, the structure of the facility dictating invention and adaptation. For example, the conventional pool has a gutter below the deck edge which normally is about eight inches from the surface of the water. This makes a sitting roll-in logical. Other pools are constructed so that the water level is flush with the gutter so that this same starting position would be awkward. It might be in this case that starting on one knee would be more sensible. Another

---

[2] The only position which is "out" altogether is one starting on *two* knees. This is very hard on the knee caps and can cause skinned shins.

Step 1—sit

Step 2—one knee

Step 3—tip-in

Step 4—fall-in

Step 5—small spring

Step 6—spring, arm coordination

position for edges very close to the water is a squatting position. This has the disadvantage of being a very difficult balance to hold. Another variation used in particular cases where the edge is exactly the right height and is smooth is what is called a seal dive, or a slip-in.

Squat dive

Seal dive

a.

b.

If one step in the progression is a real stumbling block, the teacher can go back to the preceding step for more confidence, or, very occasionally, can skip and go ahead. The general idea is that for the beginner, the closer he is to the water the safer he feels. It is true that the closer he is, the less slap he will feel should he make a mistake. At the same time, it is harder to accomplish a dive within the smaller distance from the water—something a beginner never quite believes.

The progression from the side is a crucial period in the learning of diving for both student and teacher. It is the time when habits are formed which can help develop excellent diving or which become faults never lost. The teacher can spot fault tendencies, which, if corrected at this very early stage, will never be problems later. If the teacher breezes through the elementary series too fast and too superficially without attention to some key techniques, he is conditioning the student to poor diving from the start.

What are the key techniques, the details which will carry over into good springboard techniques? First is FOCUS: the eyes must be open—seeing and judging from the very first roll-in. Closely related to the focus is the working together of the head, arms, and shoulders. The beginner should "sit tall," and stretch arms overhead in line with his ears. Then bend forward (without losing balance), stopping here: Now see that arms and head are still in line, and that eyes look beyond the fingers to a point in the water below approximately eighteen inches from the pool side. The student should actually see the under side of his fingers, not the top of his hands. Then the student rolls in, trying not to let his fingers slide out or under, but maintaining his aim on an imaginary fixed point in the water. He rolls in, should let himself straighten out as he feels natural, lift his head and come up when he feels he is all in. As he repeats these roll-ins, he can try to go deeper and deeper.

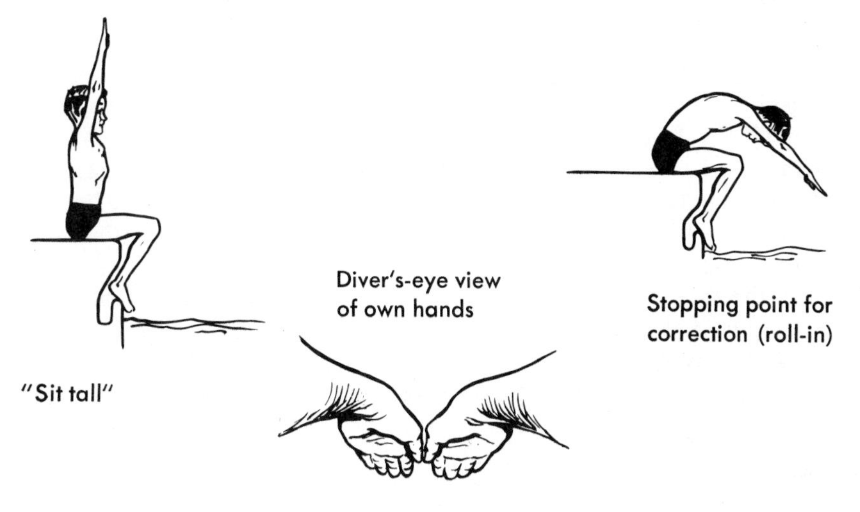

"Sit tall"

Diver's-eye view of own hands

Stopping point for correction (roll-in)

The beginner may feel that he will hurt his eyes hitting the water. For the teacher's assurance and the diver's too, here are the facts: we all have a winking reflex which causes our eyes to blink when faced with any unusual environmental factor such as strong wind, foreign irritation, *and* entering water. This reflex is extremely fast, and being a reflex, we don't have to remember to close our eyes—it is automatic.

The key techniques which we began segregating here, then, are to *look for the entry point,* to *keep the arms in line with the head,* to *allow the body to unfold from flexion into extension,* and *to hold the entry under water.* Here are some obvious things which happen when these techniques are ignored:

Hands slid out, eyes closed

Lifted head from start: "belly flop"

Did not unroll: "jump-dive"

Lifted head under water—very hard on back

Rolled over, eyes closed; came up "lost", with headful of water

In any of the first four steps of the progression, all of these faults are usually the same as illustrated, and are caused by approximately the same things. In the one-knee position, beginners sometimes push too hard with the foot and cause various aberrations such as shoving themselves straight out or flipping over. Failure to rotate at all, to remain in the rolled up position, happens mostly in the first two steps (sitting and kneeling). A little practice with handstands, against the wall, in the gym, or in the shallow end of the pool, often helps teach the right combination of rotation and unfolding.

As the diver stands straighter he enters the water with more force, and it becomes more and more important for him to control his body rotation by holding with the abdominal muscles just before entry. Even at an early stage this can be learned.

Step 3, the TIP-IN, has several individual characteristics. The forward position must be assumed with the weight mostly on one foot, the other just behind. The weight now being over the ball of the forward foot, the back leg begins to extend from the hip. The focus, arm, and head position are stable. As the lifting leg begins to cause a real loss of balance, the arms stretch harder toward the entry point and guide the diver in. Legs meet at entry. The back leg must not be kicked or pressed back beyond the vertical line of the body.

Tip-in series (Step 3)

Step 4, the FALL-IN, seems hard for most beginners when they first try it. It doesn't feel as though the legs would follow in line with the head and arms. If the beginner does not quite trust the instructions given (bend over, set entry point, keep knees straight, fall in), he may add a few ideas of his own. The two most frequent and erroneous ideas are to *kick* the legs, which from the forward starting position will flip his legs nicely over (b), or to quit on the way to the water by "pulling" his knees, thereby giving himself a slap on the thighs (c). Occasionally a beginner "freezes" at the hip joint (d).

The fall-in is very important. It should be accomplished with ease, control, and conviction before a straight standing start is tried. The body position on entry should be reasonably good: legs straight, feet together, total body position firm and stretched. The beginner should be able to take this fall-in right to the bottom of the pool or lake, assuming there is seven to ten feet of water. He should be instructed on the proper technique for landing on the bottom (see p. 36).

Fall-in faults

Step 5, SMALL SPRING from a straight standing position, is a debatable one. In a group which works fast and easily, it could be omitted. For the ones having difficulty, and for older pupils, the "small spring" is a little gentler transition from the fall-in to the completed dive. Two new factors come with this step: first, the diver stands erect, which may make him a bit apprehensive about the greater distance to the water; second, he is going to push actively from his feet for the first time. This should be a slight push, just a bend-stretch feeling, the head and shoulders pulling over as he stretches. Coaching for a slight loss of balance before the push will eliminate any chance of coming close to the side, and will make the rotation easier to accomplish. Coaching for a fairly *quick* bend-stretch will help keep the body in line.

Standing dive with small spring (Step 5)

Actually teaching a small lean before the spring is a controversial point. Many repudiate the thought of ever *teaching* lean since most divers lean far more than necessary anyway, especially beginners. A justification for teaching lean is to begin to teach an awareness of balance and balance change. If the student can learn to feel and to control exactly his total change in balance in this early stage, he can go far. Judgment of one's changing balance is a large part of the art of diving.

At this point the beginner can also learn the difference between a lean and a bend. Bending involves no loss of balance and will only make it more difficult to spring. For Step 5 the lean should be very slight, just a beginning of balance loss, followed very quickly by the knee-ankle flexion-extension.

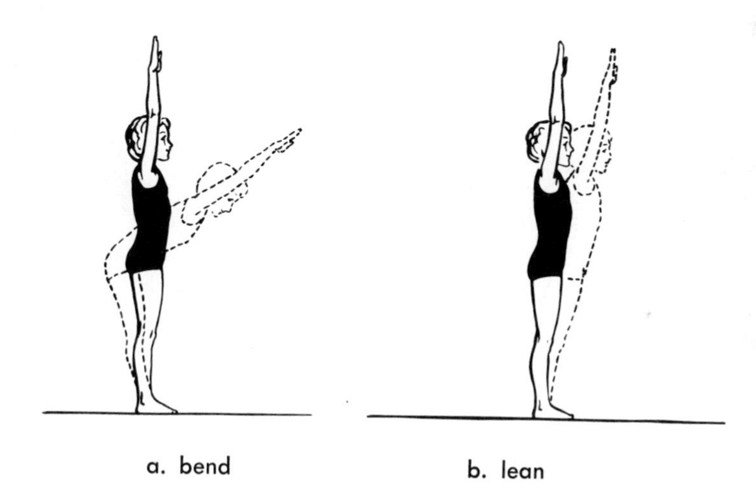

a. bend b. lean

Why set the head and arms in such a static position from start to finish in Step 5? The arm action is left out so as to eliminate one factor of concentration, the spring of the legs from a vertical position being the first vital point. The head and arms are set at the beginning as they will be for the entry. In this set position with the arms overhead throughout, the student can also better feel and learn the body action as a whole without a confusing and inept flailing of the arms. The rotation of the body is achieved by a slight lean, by arm and shoulder stretch after takeoff toward the entry point, with arms, head, and body in alignment all the way.

The standing dive with small spring will go wrong if the lean is at all exaggerated, causing the student to overthrow. All the faults common to the preceding steps can enter in, plus a tendency for beginners to kick the legs over with the spring. One does not *force* the legs up and over, but learns to push down directly underneath oneself, then to guide the resulting force at other end with head, arms, and shoulders. The feet will follow—they are attached!

Step 6, SPRING WITH ARM COORDINATION, adds the use of the arms as an accompanying and augmenting action which goes along with the general body action of Step 5. Lean, as a coaching point, is ordinarily left out of the picture by now. The forward direction of the arm action is enough to guide the body balance forward, and an emphasis or even mention of lean is apt to be taken too seriously by the student. The coordination of the arms here is a lateral press—vertical lift action which is essentially the same for all takeoffs on the springboard, forward or backward.

Takeoff push coordination

In addition to the same balance, alignment, and entry of the dive for which we have been working all along, we add the arm lift and stretch *into* the set position of Step 5; then over the top in an arc and to the water. "Climb over the hill and slide down the other side." The arm lift preceding the body extension is a forceful movement from a low position into an overhead position. Whether the arms move through a forward-upward arc fairly straight, or whether the elbows bend on the way, is immaterial. The former is perhaps a little more graceful, but the action is quick, and some divers more naturally fall into the more vertical elbow flexion-extension.

New faults creeping in at this stage have to do with the arm direction, lack of force, or lack of alignment in the dive. Most of these faults are seen as arm faults and often can be corrected by an emphasis on arm

Straight arm lift

Elbow flexion arm lift

stretch in the right direction. However the basic rotation and alignment faults always involve the entire body's muscular control. So check and re-emphasize the action taking place elsewhere if arm correction alone does not seem to be effective.

Arm action faults during flight

a. partial arm lift

b. incomplete arm extension

c. arm lift, followed by too sharp a pull to the water

d. breast-stroking action of arms

7

Beginning on the Board— Forward Dive

A. FALL-IN

The "fall-in" is the best practice for learning control of additional height from the water and eliminating all factors of spring. It should be used in all situations for the first springboard lesson of any class, beginning through advanced. Many who call themselves advanced have never learned fall-in control. This is a basic step for beginners, and constant good entry review for competitors.

The procedure for the fall-in from the board is basically the same as for the fall-in from the side of the pool: walk to the end of the board; bend over and touch ankles, keeping the knees straight; move hands out from the end of the board about a foot; look at the water just over the the hands; then lean forward toward the water, holding the focus and the fingertip position at a fixed spot (entry point), and fall in.

The difference between the fall-in from the board and the fall-in from the side of the pool is the greater height from the water. This greater distance to be traveled through the air means a longer period of body control, a greater impact on hitting the water, thus a stronger abdominal control and body extension through the entry phase and

Fall-in

underwater position. Bottom should be reached in a straight line without difficulty. Be sure it is a true fall-in without any spring whatsoever. In this starting position, bent over at the hips, any spring at all will cause overthrow. An easy check on this for the teacher is to watch for board vibration as the diver leaves it.

Begin to watch for and correct the maintenance of focus and body line from the beginning of the fall. Are the eyes open? (If the teacher stands diagonally behind the board tip, he can see the student's eyes throughout.) Do the fingertips maintain a fixed angle or do they move in or out, making the student swing over or land flat? Has the student the body control to fall into extension from the flexed hip position without continuing into over-extension? Do the knees remain straight, or do they collapse on impact? Is the body truly aligned on entry into the water? Is the position held under water or relaxed too soon?

ENTRY FAULTS

Hands slide out, dive shallow

Hands slide under, dive over

Over-extension at hip joint, arched entry

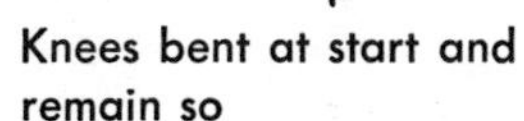

Knees bent at start and remain so

Tense hip joint, remains in flexion

Knees relaxed at point of entry

Over-extension at hip joint, plus relaxed knees

Specific head position
a. chin up—face slapped
b. chin down—back of head slapped
c. arms over ears—correct entry alignment

IMPORTANT: When students are asked how a diver should enter the water (at what angle), they answer almost without exception, "Straight," meaning at 90 degrees to the water. THIS IS NOT TRUE. Every dive has a degree of rotation.[3] If a diver lands on the water "straight," he will always continue moving slightly in the direction of the rotation, causing the dive to go over.

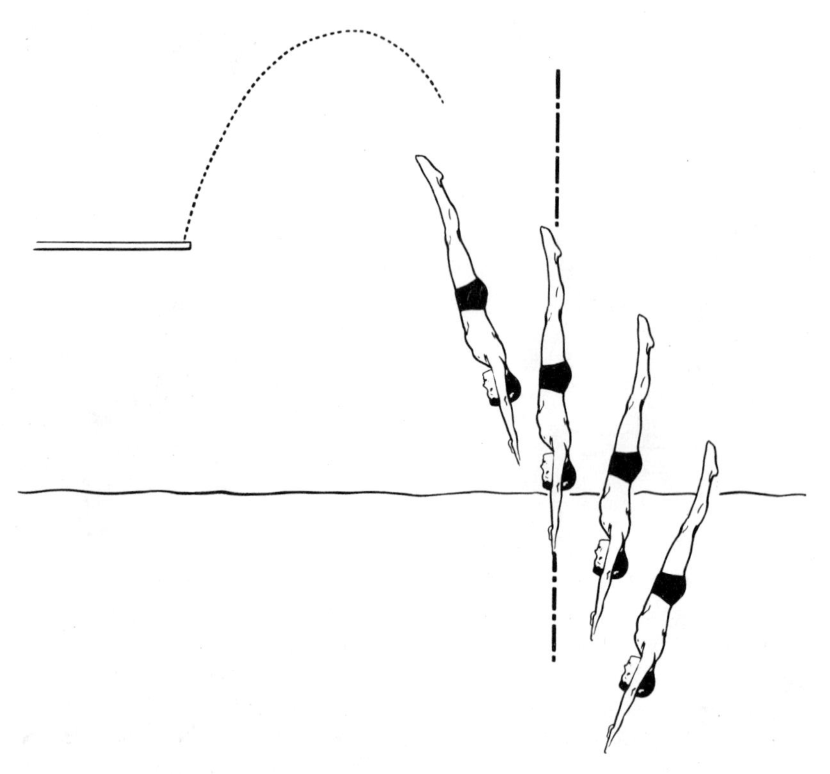

What happens to "vertical" entry

Therefore the diver must aim *short* of vertical—to him, about 80 degrees. As he falls, he will ride an arc and will go into the same hole in the water which his hands make. To the spectator the whole thing takes place in split seconds and it will *appear* that the diver is going in an at 90 degrees. This feeling of playing it slightly "short" on all entries should be taught

---

[3] See Chapter 3, pp. 17–19.

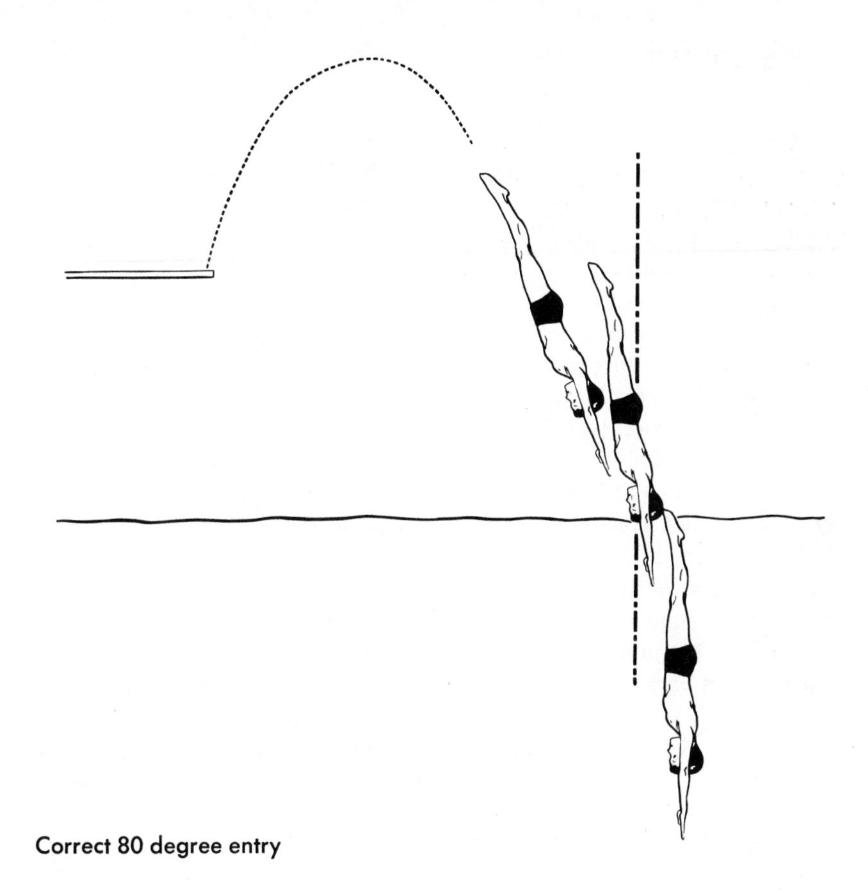

Correct 80 degree entry

from the beginning. All divers must be taught to plan their entries with this in mind, starting with the first fall-ins.

The beginning teacher and the beginning student are apt to be over-conscious of the position of the legs and feet during entries. Much effort is put into trying to keep knees straight, feet together, and toes pointed. These are important points in dive appearance and in alignment control, yet generally secondary to takeoff balance, control of body position from its center, and entry aim. *To demand perfection of entry in the exacting details of foot and leg position for the beginner means to stress details before the body as a whole is under control.*

However, the fall-in from the board offers an ideal situation for the beginnings of entry control, and the fall-in can be returned to often for continued entry practice. The knees should be straight in line with the body. This can be consciously felt in the strong thigh contraction and the stretch at the back of the knee joint. There is a reciprocal reaction that if the ankles are strongly extended and the toes pointed, the knees will automatically extend. It is not reciprocal that the feet should be held together side by side. This takes a separate concentration of feeling the heels and the big toes touching all the way through the water. To the expert "feet apart" is any time that the feet are not touching each other. From the point of takeoff through entry in *all* dives the feet should be together, so eventually this action of slightly squeezing the feet must be completely automatic.

Small boys, and many others, have much trouble with this feet-together business. A most successful gimmick is to have them practice falling in with something held between their feet. Pencils, bathing caps, and pieces of rubber are good. A dollar bill held between the toes almost never slips out. Thereafter the students pretend they are holding the item.

For beginners and intermediates in group classes, the teacher must keep moving and not expect perfection, nor wait for perfection. What he must look for are the beginnings of control and sensitivity to position. If the line of the dive is fairly good; if the control of focus, body position, knees, and toes is good; if depth attained is passable, then the diver should move on to the next phase. Always be ready, however, to hold the slower moving ones back: nothing is gained by going on to a step yet harder to control.

The more skilled should be made to perfect this fall-in from any board height. A point of difficulty here is the general attitude that this is beginning stuff and beneath the notice of the fancy diver. It is *not* only beginning stuff, but a means to learning the accuracies of entry control and entry position.

These details of entry faults have been taken up in relation to the fall-in, and will not be repeated in connection with standing and running dives. The faults are frequently caused by the same factors in the other dives, so the reader should return to these illustrations for reference. Other influences come into effect with the addition of approach and spring, but many old fall-in faults may merely be exaggerated by the greater physical force of the diver and additional components of force.

B. STANDING DIVE

This is included in springboard progression to introduce the beginner to a start on the board from the vertical position. Now he must learn to give the board impetus, to ride his small impetus in an arc and still control his flight and his entry. The standing dive is very difficult, starting from nothing more than a slight flexion-extension at hips, knees, and ankles. The initial inertia is hard to overcome. Therefore, it is recommended that this stage be only a brief transition between the fall-in and the learning of the approach steps—as brief as possible, with only a modicum of success necessary.

Standing straight on the end of the board, the student places arms about waist high to the side and looks at what he considers his correct entry point. With a downward press of the arms, he bends his knees and pushes the board, riding up and away with an arm reach and body extension. A very short arc can be made and then he must concentrate on stretching to his entry point. Ideally, there should be no body flexion during the flight in the air; this being practically impossible, there is usually a slight hip flexion and a very strong shoulder pull over the top of the arc.

Standing dive

Watch for tendencies to kick or flip feet from the beginning of the spring. The force of the flexion-extension should go straight down. The great fault of all beginners is to lose balance forward preceding the spring and thus flip over or be carried too far out. The distance necessary for the dive is controlled largely by the up-over direction of arms and shoulders, and easily so. Lean *per se* does not have to be coached unless the student has a cut back tendency due to incomplete spring (see p. 71).

C. FORWARD APPROACH

The dive proper being what can be accomplished between the end of the board and the water, the approach, or "boardwork," consists of those things done in preparation for this flight. There are few absolute rules governing these things other than those of common sense and best efficiency. Leeway can be allowed for all the individual differences of weight, height, sex, build, and idiosyncrasy.

In the forward approach the rules for competition are at least three steps, a spring off one foot to the end of the board (hurdle), and a two-foot takeoff from there. The whole should be executed smoothly. In a recreational situation, one can make one's own rules—be as lenient or unorthodox as one likes—but the advantages of following the competitive pattern relate to possible future use for the diver. The rather specific pattern came about because over the years it has been found to be the most conducive to good diving.

1. ONE-STEP APPROACH

The difficult part of the approach is the hurdle, which is the key to balance, control, and height of the dive. Yet it has been my experience that to teach the hurdle in minute and exact detail to the beginner is rarely successful. It is more frequently confusing and discouraging. I like to sneak up on the beginner, to oversimplify the procedure with the hope of leading him into it naturally and establishing his individual rhythm and movement pattern. This is my method:

a) Start two walking steps behind the board tip.
b) Take a step on one foot, land on two at the tip (first step halving the distance to the end of the board).
c) Dive in, without breaking the continuity of motion.

Say no more. Do not clutter the coaching with specific arm or knee or body movements. General coaching may help, such as to let the arms do what they want to do; try to keep balance straight over the board tip; keep the arc of the dive up and over as in the standing dive; keep the jump (the beginning hurdle) at least a step long; land on both feet at once.

When the beginner can do this fairly smoothly, introduce the idea of raising his arms as he steps so that the arms will be up and to the side in a position to press down with the body as it drops to the tip. This is the identical position as at the start of the standing dive. Focus should be on the board tip throughout the step and the jump. Here a little practice on looking down the nose and yet remaining as straight as possible will help.

One-step approach

A split second before contact is made between the toes and the board the eyes should look straight ahead in order to set the alignment of the head straight over the shoulders. As the takeoff push is in process the eyes should be directed upward momentarily in line with the desired angle of takeoff. From the top of the arc of flight the focus should be concentrated on the entry point.

A most valuable exercise, especially for those who lean forward at or before takeoff, is to work on this one-step approach without actually diving off. Instead, take a spring in place on the board tip. This will be impossible to do if there is any degree of lean. The approach and single bounce exercise is far better for the diver than continuous bouncing. On the negative side, the diver who works a great deal on the approach and single bounce may form the habit of making his spring too straight when he means to dive. He may also begin balking at the end of the board, procrastinating until he gets the spring which feels exactly right. Therefore the exercise should be interrupted from time to time at the teacher's direction and discretion rather than practiced constantly.

2. THREE-STEP APPROACH

So far we have the one-step approach, being actually one step and a jump off that foot to the end of the board. As in the case of the standing dive, this one-step stage is artificial, hard to intiate with no building up of motion, and false in terms of eventual rhythm and continuity of motion.

When the beginner has the feeling of the one-step and a degree of control and understanding, move right on to the full three-step approach before boredom sets in. And do not expect perfection with the takeoff from one step: only experts have the control and strength to dive with height and grace from such a small windup.

To start the full approach, again keep it very simple:

a) Take three walking steps.
b) Hop off the third step.
c) Land on the end on two feet.
d) Dive.

Three-step approach

Keep building on what has already been experienced: fall-ins for basic entry control and learning the focus; standing dives for initial spring feeling plus flight through the air; one-step approach for relating a step-jump to the board tip to the air. Now the three-step approach for a longer, stronger, smoother transition to the hurdle and takeoff.

Continue to stay away as much as possible from details: no coaching on arms, toes, or position of hurdle. The only essentials are smooth, easy steps; a hurdle at least as long as a normal walking step; and fair balance on the takeoff. Let the rest of the details grow within the natural movement of the diver.

Which foot should one start with? In the one-step approach the coaching is to start with whichever foot feels natural. As this is practiced the beginner should be aware of which foot feels best to push from into the hurdle. Often the teacher may have the group stand on the deck and hop several times on each foot to determine which is their best "jumping leg" respectively. There is no law about one's preference here, any more than there is about being right- or lefthanded.

Proceeding to the three-step approach the diver should start with the same foot as he started with in the one-step approach. In the first weeks the novice may change off experimentally, but soon should form the habit of using the same foot in order to develop his hurdle on his good side. The starting foot may later be switched: sometimes the diver has guessed wrong on which *is* his good takeoff foot for the hurdle. Also the coach may try the change when a diver gets stale and needs a new challenge.

How does one set the length of these first approaches? The diver can stand with his back to the water at the tip, then measure his steps and hurdle going away from the water; or he can take a guess and adjust according to results. His starting position will have to be adjusted as he improves, but eventually should be set. Even so, experienced divers are constantly shifting their starting points in accordance with board pitch or flexibility.

The completed running[4] front dive is now practiced—smooth steps; easy hurdle with general upswing of arms; landing at tip, and continuing without break into press; takeoff stretching arms upward; focus on entry point (80 degrees); guiding dive up, over, and down to the bottom. Hard to control, this simple arc, yet we must start here because of its simplicity.

[4] "Running" is a misnomer. It is a slightly accelerated walk.

8

Boardwork Details

The fine points of boardwork should not be stressed or even explained to the beginner. He will not be able to comprehend so much at once, much less apply it, and all this information may even be detrimental to his progress. As the teacher sees where certain fine points can be introduced, particularly in forestalling faulty habits, he can begin to teach the more exact movements of effective boardwork. Thus the teacher should be aware of the fine points of boardwork and of all the implications of these in producing good diving without presenting them to a group all at once as an indigestible lump. Serve when needed.

No diver's boardwork is ever perfect, and no two divers look exactly alike in their boardwork mechanics. Some get admirable results from unorthodox form. The material following is culled from experience and observation as a personal analysis of standards toward which to work.

A. THE THREE STEPS

Why exactly three steps? The rulebooks say at *least* three, so a diver may take four or five steps if he so desires. Most take three or four, the choice being primarily a rhythmic preference—simply that one rhythm *feels* better than the other. Some think a four-step approach, using more of the board's length, lends a smoother, more flowing aspect to the movement. It also provides the diver with an extra step for building up force for the hurdle. The three-step approach is simpler: the takeoff step into the hurdle being the third one, the diver starts his walk on the same foot as he does with his one-step hurdle. A fourth step can be added later to see if the diver is happier with the longer approach.

The steps should be normal heel and toe walking steps, accelerating slightly in speed and length. This can be taught by walking normally on the pool deck and then carrying the walk right into practice approaches. The body should be as erect as possible within a slight total forward balance; the diver should watch the board tip from the beginning of his walk. There should be a strong press from the ball of the foot into each step without destroying the smoothness of total forward motion. Walk a little faster than is comfortable.

Arm movement accompanying the steps should be minimal and functional—no breast stroking down the board! The two movement pattern possibilities are a slight arm swing in opposition as in walking, or a small parallel swing. As the step into the hurdle (third step) is taken, the arms

Correct arm action into hurdle

should be behind the body line in preparation for the hurdle lift. This third step is the same as the others, with a little more force as a result of the preceding steps.

STEP FAULTS

A common fault is a jump or stamp into the third step, which is the takeoff point for the hurdle. It occurs when a diver anticipates the hurdle and puts too much emphasis too soon on the downward action preceding it. This sets up board vibrations which disturb the timing of the normal landing from the hurdle a second later. It also interrupts the smooth motion of the diver, may put him off balance going into the hurdle, and lessens his elevation potential. A heel-toe sequence into strong leg extension is absolutely necessary for complete leg strength use in gaining elevation.

Fault: jump into third step

Fault: over-reach and low body position, third step

Almost all divers will over-reach in the third step in trying for the hurdle. Try to have them walk as normally as possible and to get the weight off that foot as soon as possible. Emphasize a quick press-LIFT into the air. Timing is important here: if the diver is a little slow to get off the third step, he will lose the momentum and force gained from the preceding steps.

Correct any uneveness in tempo or length of step. The clue here is not only visual but also auditory—the *sound* of varying rhythm, of uneven pressure, of a heavy walk. Watch for poor general walking mechanics such as the weight too long or too hard on the heels, sinking into the hip joint, shoulder dropping to the sides, shoulder stiffness or elevation, walking with feet wide apart, "duck walking" (toes out), or "pigeon toeing." Faults in posture and in the use of the feet will certainly influence the efficiency and balance of the boardwork. The head, as a heavy mass over the moving body and perhaps affected by visual concentration forward, is often the prime offender in body alignment when walking. Consciousness of an erect head and neck, notwithstanding a focus on the tip of the board, must be practiced and practiced.

Overuse of arm movement accompanying the steps is very common. Beginners seem to feel a need for, and security in, swinging the arms—an idea that the harder they can swing, circle, and push the arms, the more power they will have. These movements are mostly wasted since elevation

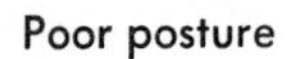

Poor posture

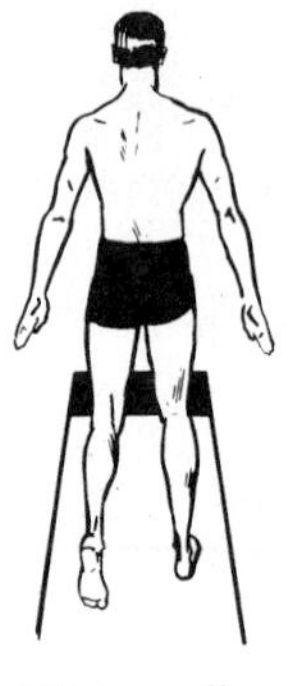

Wide walk

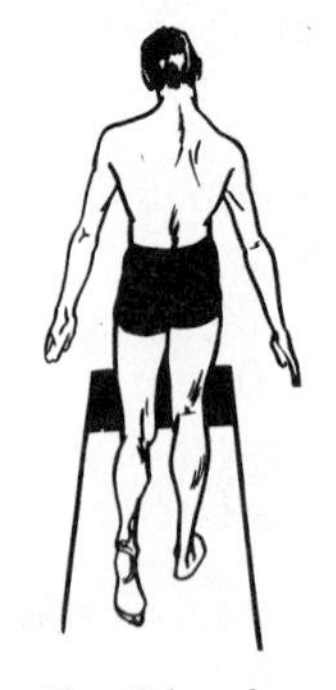

Shoulder drop

power lies mainly in the legs as the weight-bearing limbs. If the unnecessary arm movements are extreme, they will interfere with balance and will prevent the legs and body from accomplishing their proper action in elevation. Watch also for unevenness in arm movement, which produces uneven landing pressures, causing twists and side leanings on takeoff.

"Breast-stroking"

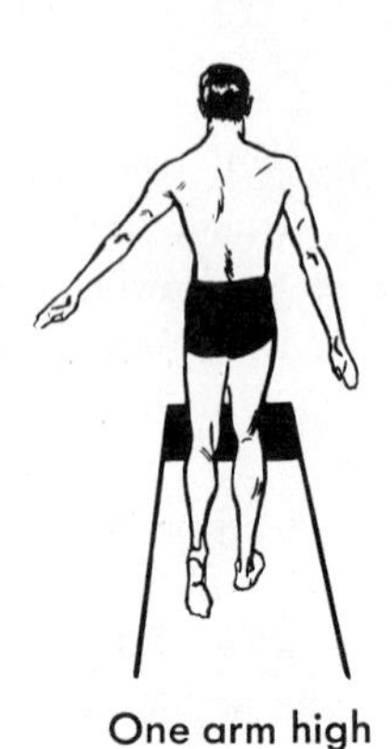

One arm high

B. THE HURDLE

The hurdle itself is initiated by a strong extension off the third step; that is, an extension of the leg carrying the weight. This is accompanied by a lift of the arms, a passing through of the other knee in a flexed position, and a strong body extension upward. The flexed knee should come through and ride at about a right angle. The pushing leg becomes straight with its strong extension and remains so until landing at the tip. Both ankles extend strongly. This is a difficult asymmetrical force and balance, and takes much practice to perfect.

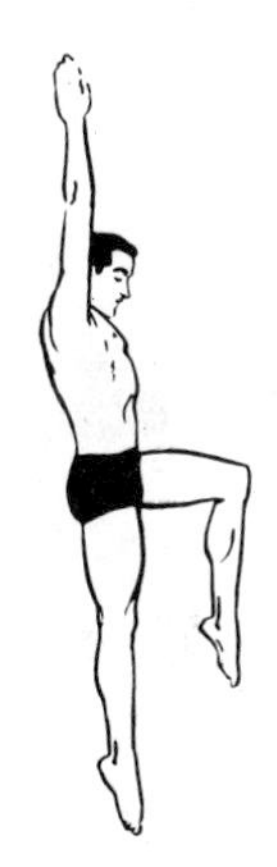
Correct position at top of hurdle

On the descent of the hurdle, now over the tip of the board, the one knee should ride flexed as long as possible and straighten out just before landing. Focus is still on the board tip, looking down the nose. The body is aligned so that the moving weight is directly over the extended leg.

For the landing press the drop to the end must be in balance. The body position must be as vertical as possible. The timing of the press is made in coordination with the board spring and in accordance with the diver's weight and strength. Contact is made with the bottom of the toes. The feet roll quickly down to the heels, knees flex considerably after contact, and the hips flex slightly. Simultaneously, the arms descend very quickly from the side overhead position to a side press position. The head now sets in alignment with the vertical body balance, and the focus is straight out.

In a split second the weight of the body has depressed the board and a strong extension of all parts follows. The diver is directed upward, with slight variations in arm and head position and in the direction of the hip lift according to the mechanics called for in that particular dive.

How much distance should the hurdle cover? Recommendations go from twelve to thirty inches. Better to make it at least as long as the diver's normal walking step, and, if possible, slightly longer. The length will vary according to the diver's height, leg strength, and foot size.

The height attained in any forward dive is in direct proportion to the height attained in the hurdle, other things being equal. How does the teacher measure height in the hurdle? He looks for the elevation attained by the *straight* leg of the hurdle. This is the leg which has just pushed off with the body weight over it, and is the part of the body finally responsible for hurdle height. Watch this leg and foot carefully in coaching for

Correct boardwork

Close-up of feet

height. Work on its strong extension in good position all the way through the toes.

HURDLE FAULTS

1. HURDLE LENGTH

First look at the actual length of the hurdle and the influence of this length on the diver's balance in the air and at the board tip. A hurdle too long for the diver will be low and ineffective, and may cause him to lean forward in order to make it to the end of the board. A very short hurdle will cause problems in handling the abrupt change in balance from forward to vertical movement.

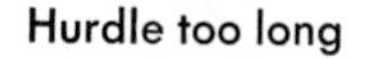

Hurdle too long

Hurdle too short

Focus control is important: the diver may keep watching the board tip too long and cause a lean. Some do not watch the tip at all, thus have no awareness of where it is or when it is coming. This will make the diver land back from the tip or overlap it. At the peak of the hurdle, the diver should be able to sight the tip along the pointed toe of his bent leg. He should be able to land within one inch of the tip.

2. HURDLE FLIGHT

Within the hurdle flight watch for deviations in the body position, particularly in the straight line which should be seen from the ears down through the hips, knee of extended leg, and ankle of extended leg. Hip flexion to some degree is a common fault, caused by incomplete leg or body extension, eagerness to get to the end, forward head, arm lift forward, or swinging forward. An arm lift too far behind the body will cause a counteracting forward position. If the arms swing continuously, they will not contribute to the landing: they will arrive at the press position *before* contact instead of *with* contact. Coach for a real stop of arm movement at the top of the hurdle spring and throughout most of the descent.

Hurdle flight faults

The flexed knee in the hurdle has a role in hurdle height as an accompanying lift, but serves primarily as a balance factor in hurdle flight. Its position is important: the knee should be centered; the foot should be directly underneath the knee, toes extended; the knee should be waist high or slightly higher, never lower. Deviations from the correct position will affect the total balance and mechanics.

Proper position and arm timing sequence—third step to peak of hurdle

Frequently the flexed knee extends to match the other one too soon, making the diver tense and off balance. Mechanics vary, but I recommend a gradual extension of the flexed knee, feet arriving together just before contact and no sooner. After the emphasis and tension of the very strong press into the hurdle, there should be a feeling of dropping as a dead weight to the end of the board just before the second strong press at the takeoff.

Hurdle faults in the flexed leg

a. flexion absent, leg straight

b. inadequate flexion, foot forward

c. knee low

d. knee high

Knee extension timing from hurdle

3. LANDING AND TAKEOFF

On landing and takeoff the feet should roll from the extended position quickly down into a push from the heel on the board to extending the toes as they leave it. An early "un-pointing" of the toes will cause a flat-footed landing. Failure to extend the toes quickly again on leaving means that the full spring potential is not used. Knees may flex too much or too little, which is primarily a timing fault, though sometimes caused by tension. The spring will be absorbed in the joints if the body is too relaxed, and if the body is too tense, spring cannot be fully utilized.

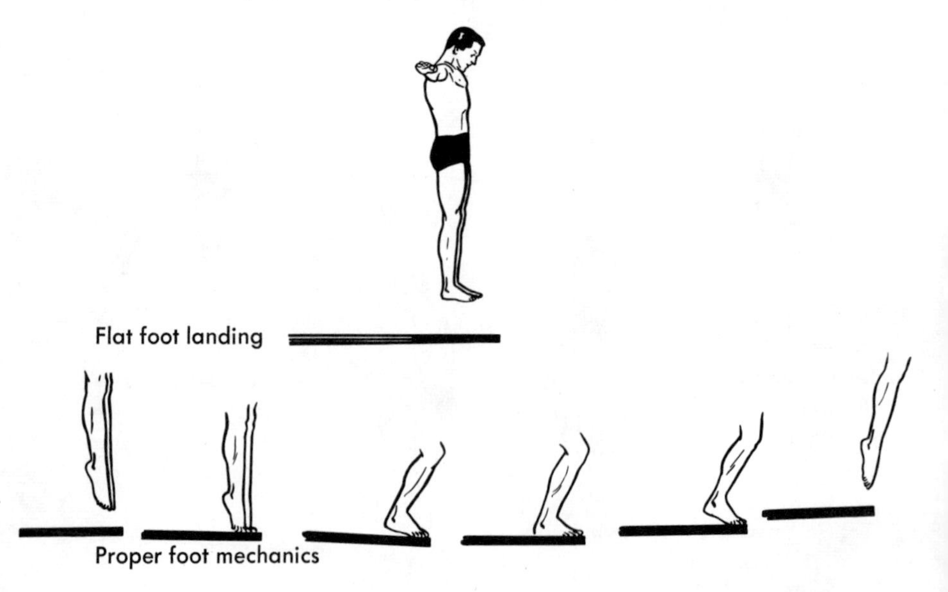

Flat foot landing

Proper foot mechanics

Balance faults almost always involve a lean forward, either caused by many preceding faults in the steps and the hurdle or because the dive is anticipated. Providing the balance on the landing *is* good, then the arm lift and body extension set the direction and tension of the takeoff, guided by correct focus upward. If the arms and upper part of the body pull over the top of the dive before the legs have completed their extension, a "cut back" will occur. This means that the diver breaks his normal dive arc by not fully utilizing the board rebound through his body. His center of gravity will tend to remain stationary, he will cut off his height and come close to the board. "Cut back" also occurs when the diver extends his legs too fast, failing to ride the board timing, and to complete his spring with the body aligned.

"Cut back"—pulling over too soon "Cut back"—extending legs too fast

Correction lies in work on feeling the spring right through the feet, with the weight over the feet, before the actual dive mechanics are started.

C. TEACHING TECHNIQUES IN BOARDWORK

1) Practice walking, stressing the importance of the proper use of the feet, how the body weight is carried in the walk, the proper head position.
2) Hurdle development exercise:
   a) Step forward and lift knee into hurdle position; bring foot back to place.
   b) Add to this a parallel arm swing: arms back slightly at the start of the step, arms lifting upward as the knee is lifted.

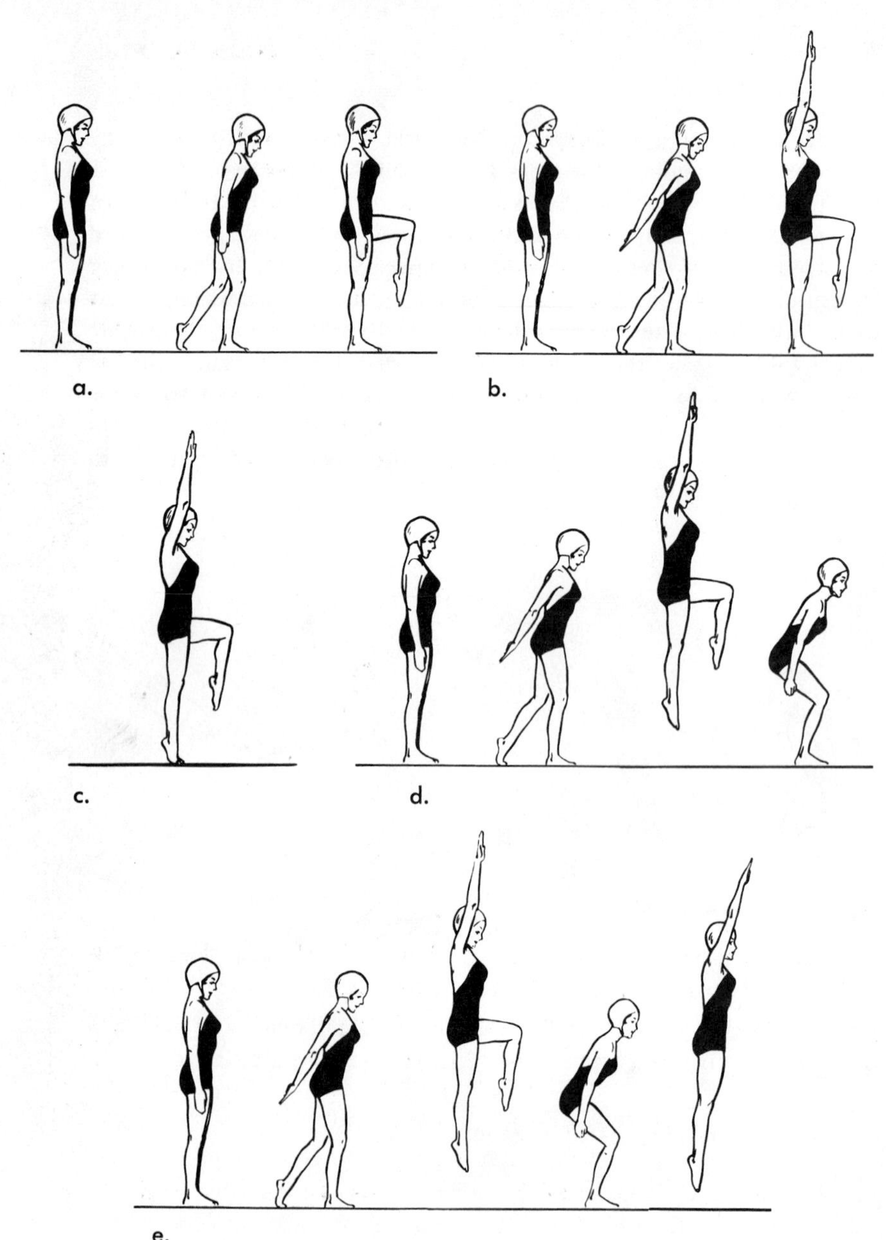

Hurdle development exercise

c) Add rising on the ball of the foot of the straight leg as the knee is lifted.

d) Practice three knee lifts followed by a fourth one taking it into a proper hurdle, and land.

e) Same as (d), with a takeoff jump added.
(Repeat each segment of the exercise many times in rhythm.)

3) Mirror practice: Work on the full approach and/or the hurdle by itself beside a long mirror and toward a long mirror.
4) Teacher take student by the hand and do many approaches with the student at his side; student match teacher in timing.
5) Teacher stand behind student, with hands on student's hips. Both take one step and a hurdle, the teacher assisting the student in the lift, giving him a longer suspension for position correction.

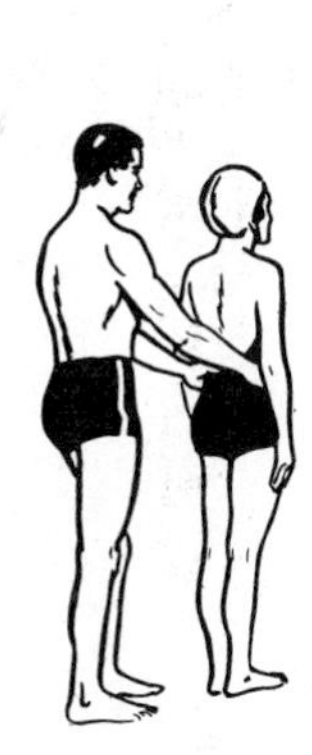
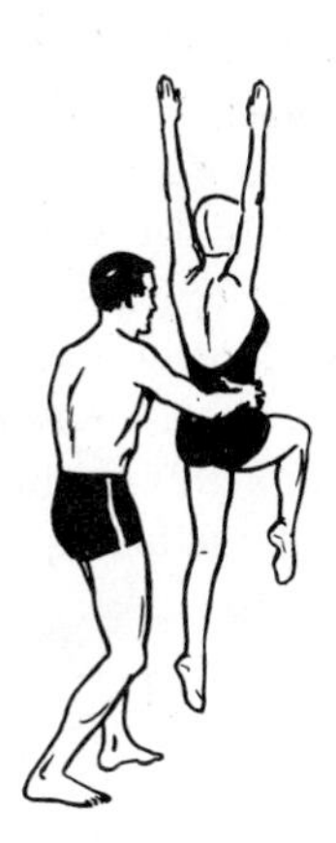

Assisted hurdle

6) Hop upstairs on one foot to strengthen the hurdle takeoff leg and foot.
7) Practice one step and a hurdle, landing on a slight elevation such as a step. Use correct form in the hurdle and try for strong extension in the straight leg.
8) Sit down with student and draw pictures of correct positions and of the faults he may have.

Hurdle practice to step

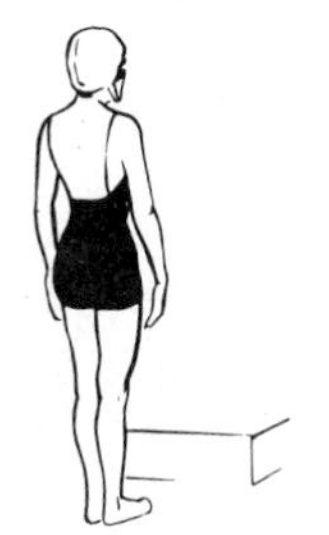
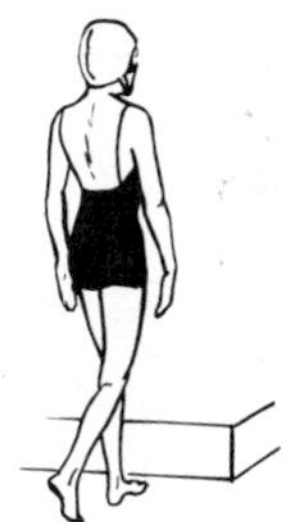

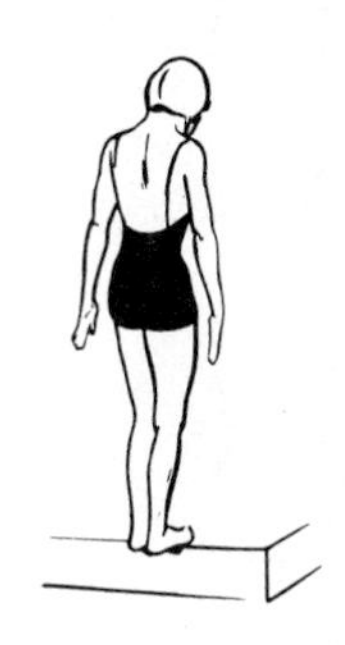

D. FUNDAMENTAL JUMPS

There is great value in learning jumps in various positions from the board. The diver can work on hurdle, takeoff, and lift without concerning himself with dive mechanics. Thus plain jumps are of great use in concentrated boardwork practice. The vertical lift of a jump is good practice for all takeoff lifts.

Beginners can be taught jumps before they are taught dives, but being conditioned only to the vertical lift, they may have difficulty adjusting to dive rotation later. The jumps are far more essential for the intermediate and advanced diver, for concentration on the fine points of boardwork and balance. They are excellent to use intermittently for a check on takeoff balance (especially for those who lean forward badly) and for getting across the idea of upward arm reach on takeoff.

The form and balance of the jump are important. A straight front jump should be a reach upward with the body in a straight line and the diver looking straight ahead. At the peak of height the arms descend quickly from the overhead position to the thighs and the diver drops into the water.

Front jump

The straight front jump is used specifically in leading up to the reverse dive (see Chapter 8) as an intermediate step between the forward and reverse directions of rotation. A straight back jump, done in the same form, is used in leading up to the inward dive (see Chapter 7). Other jumps which may be used for practice in positions and techniques are the front jump tuck, front jump pike, front jump half twist, front jump pike half twist, back jump tuck, back jump pike, and back jump half twist. For playing follow-the-leader or as a challenge to a class, these are excellent to use. Watch for overdoing them however. In these jump variations the diver is assuming positions without rotation in any direction, which can be bad conditioning for spins.

9

The Back Dive

The back dive seems logical to teach next since it is the other basic direction for the diver to learn. Some instructors teach advanced forward dives before the back dive; others feel the back dive should be started very early. There really is no set rule. In fact one could learn the back dive first of all since the movement and feeling is unrelated to the front dive. Many beginners who are very poor in their front dives take easily to back dive direction, and this is very encouraging to their interest.

A. BACK FALL-IN

The first stage is to learn the feeling of going backward in space, of entering the water upside down and backward, and of following through in this direction without getting a "headful" [5] of water. The easiest starting point is a back fall-in.

1) Student stands with heels flush with the board tip, arms extended overhead, hands together, looking straight ahead. Teacher faces student and checks that he is standing erect, arms in line with the head, no back arch. The student's arms should be stretched.

[5] "headful"—a backing up of water in nasal and sinus regions which is most uncomfortable.

Assisted back fall-in

2) Assure student that all he has to do is to lift his chin, reach back with head and arms, look for the water. *Fall,* do not spring. Keep the head slightly back. After the entry, continue in a back somersault direction underwater.
3) Check that the chin is back as the student begins to fall; keep your other hand at his back.
4) Shift both hands to diver's back; give with him as he falls; let him drop in.

Assisted back fall-in sequence

Let the student initiate the fall—never push him physically. Brace your own legs and keep your balance low. The placement of the teacher is not only to guide the student and to give him confidence, but many times to keep the student's weight going in a backward direction. It happens frequently that the novice puts his head back, bends his knees a little too much, shifts his center of gravity forward with the knee bend, and falls very close to the board:

Hip shift forward

This particular fault of shifting forward is really a fear-of-going-backward reaction. A little hand pressure at the hip by the teacher can prevent the forward shift, and just the teacher's physical presence in front of the diver may inhibit the tendency.

Hand position at hips

As the student falls he may not reach back and under enough to keep riding a circle. If his balance is not "back" enough, this may happen:

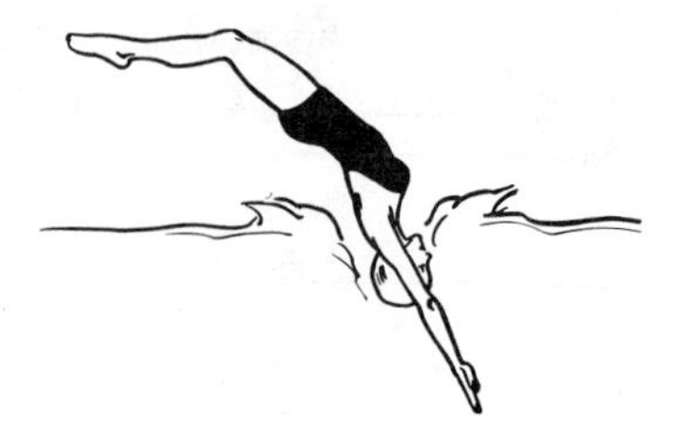

Flat entry, knee drop

and he will get a slap on the back of the legs. Here the teacher on the board can shift the hands from the small of the back down the legs as the student falls, and pick up the legs if this seems necessary:

Teacher lifting legs

The diver's movement should be followed, not initiated for him; the help given to lift the legs should be an easy lift: a strong, sudden push will flip the student over.

What else can happen in the process of the back fall-in? If the diver ducks, tucking his chin, either on the way or at the point of entry, he will slap the back of his shoulders and get a headful of water. If he ducks *under* water he will merely get a headful. The teacher's check on this is to see that the diver continues in a loop all the way around under water:

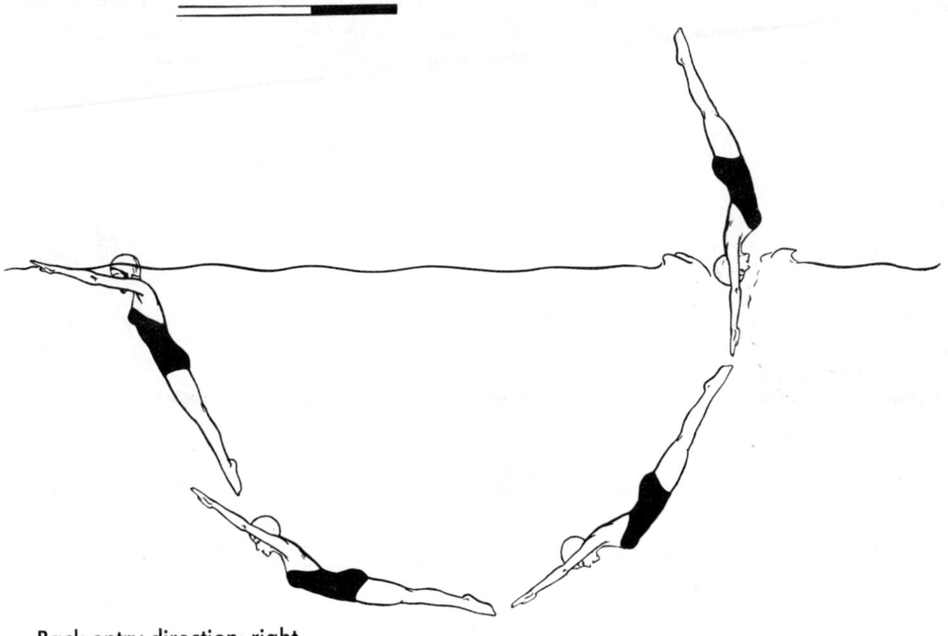

Back entry direction: right

Back entry direction: wrong

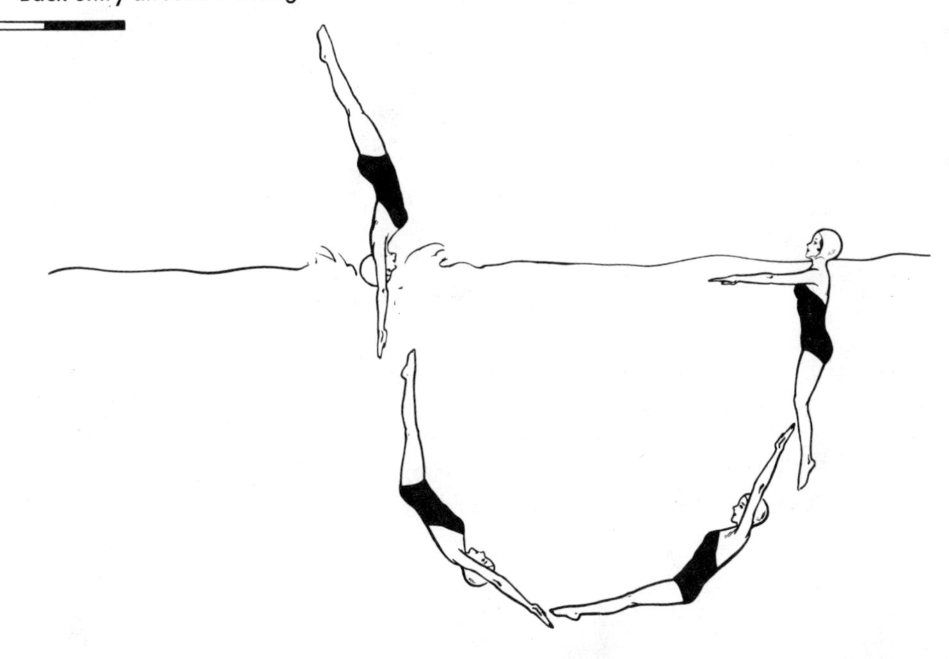

If the diver is very tense and stiff, he may not go far enough in his original pull and will land shallow. If he is very flexible in back extension and pulls hard, he may pull right over onto his stomach. This back fall-in is not a backbend. Technically it is a back extension with a strong thoracic arch and a minimum of lumbar arch.

a. Lumbar arch: wrong b. Too stiff: wrong c. Thoracic arch: right

Body positions

When the head pulls back farther than the line of the arms, the face will get slapped:

Head "out" on back entry

When the diver complains of sharp hits on the head, it is usually because arms and hands are not together (for either front or back entries):

a. arms open: wrong

b. arms closed: right

Entry

The teacher should always guide the first back fall-in, and several more, until he feels that the diver is at home and relaxed with it. Gradually he can simply let go without following the fall with his hands. Then he should stand back and let the student do it alone, with coaching as needed. The beginner should keep to these fall-ins until they are consistent and comfortable to him. He should be coached to carry them deeper into the water, to the bottom if possible.

Bottom landing, back entry

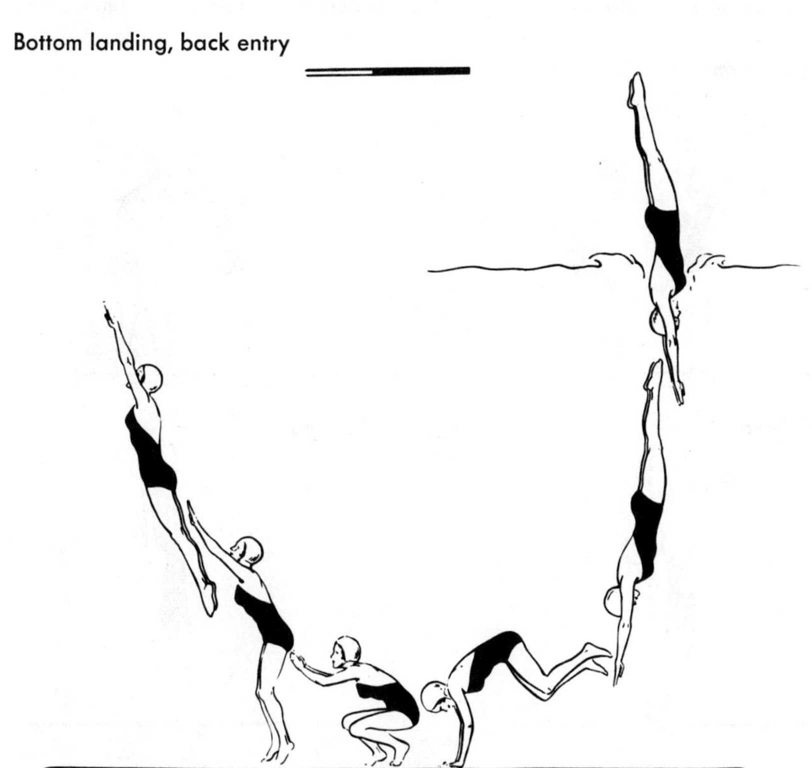

B. INITIAL BACK SPRING

Now we have to relearn the start of this back motion in order to spring safely. If the beginner were to put his head back, arch, and then spring (a sequence similar to his back fall-in), he would go far past the back dive and would likely come close to the board. The initial step for the spring can be taught in this way: stand with arms overhead, lean back slightly (head in line), bend and stretch knees quickly into the back dive position (head going back). The arm position overhead from the start is in order to eliminate arm action completely. It permits the diver to *feel* his balance better, to feel exactly what his body as a whole is doing.

The slight lean at the start is primarily a safety factor. With the lean the beginner cannot possibly hit the board. The lean must be slight, and is needed for beginners even though it must be unlearned later. The easiest way to teach this lean is on land. Taking partners, one stands behind the other, hands behind shoulders. The partner in front falls back, not far, but enough to lose balance. He should feel like a stick of wood—fall back straight from the heels. Practice this, trying to sense just when the loss of balance occurs. Also learn the difference between this lean and a back arch.

"Fall" exercise

Procedure for the first try on the board:

1) Stand erect, arms overhead. Look straight ahead, heels flush with the end of the board.
2) Lean—a "ghost" of a lean—but feel the slight loss of balance.
3) Quick bend-stretch at the knees. On the stretch, raise the chin, pull back slightly with the arms, look for the water.

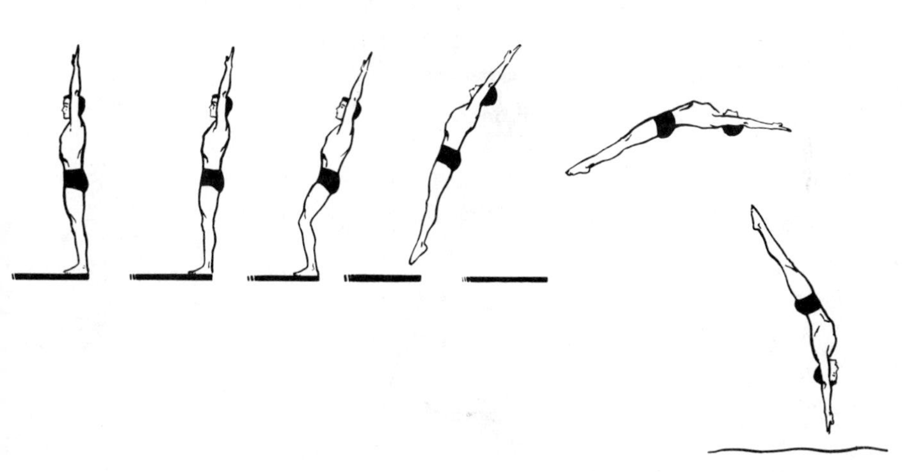

Initial back spring

The results will have to be coached as seen—for more push, more or less lean, eyes open and looking, arms in line with the body, more or less head pull. Just one caution: keep the spring gentle at first, but quick in timing.

When the initial back spring has been mastered, then it's time to move the heels back off the board and to learn the standard back takeoff.

C. STANDARD BACK TAKEOFF

Moving the heels off the board at the start means that the full flexibility of the foot can be used. The heel should drop slightly lower than the board level in its press. Here is what occurs in foot action in the process of the back takeoff:

Foot action accompanying arm swing

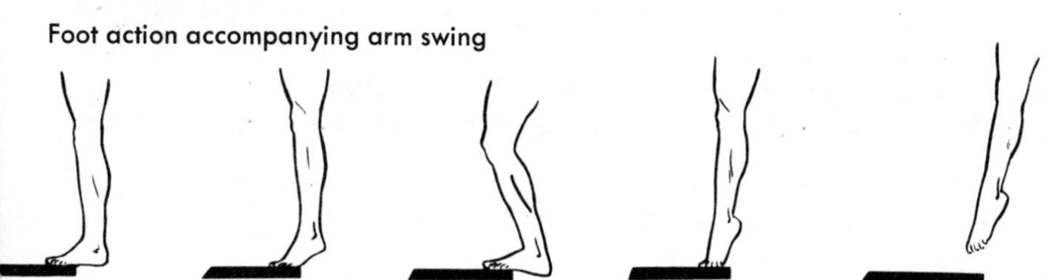

The entire ball of the foot should be on the board, including the joint between the little toe and the foot (head of the fifth metatarsal). Less than this on the board means too little purchase on the board and a chance of slipping on the press.

a. result of feet being too far off board

Too much foot on the board means that as the foot presses, its action will be checked by the board hitting the arch of the foot.

b. result of feet being too far forward on board

The arm swing for takeoff is a fairly standardized pattern: a starting stance for balance and collection of thoughts; a lift, a press, and a second lift leaving the board. Here is a step by step description:

1) Stand with back to water. Set one foot in place.
2) Place arms straight ahead, shoulder height, shoulder distance apart.
3) Set second foot.
4) Lower arms to sides.
   Pause.
5) Lift arms sideward-upward above shoulder height, lifting heels with the upward movement; toes maintain contact with board.
6) Without pause, press arms to side. Knees, hips, and ankles flex in the press action.
7) Stretch arms up and slightly back, along with leg and body extension.

If the diver swings without stop from the stationary position to the takeoff, he tends to throw himself off balance. The pause after Step 4 helps to prevent this, and is a good moment for the diver to check his balance. The arm lift which follows must be lateral; stable body balance is actually

Back stance and arm swing

maintained until Step 7—the actual takeoff. In coaching, an interesting check for balance is to have the diver practice a partial back swing, stopping at the peak of his arm lift before the press (5). He should be able to keep his balance at that point. If a lean tendency is there, he will fall in.

Individuals will vary in the rhythm of the arm swing, but the first lift (5) should be easy and steady. The press which follows (6) should be faster and more powerful. If the arm lift is overemphasized, or if there is long delay at the peak of the arm lift, balance and alignment suffer. The overemphasis can also cause "crow-hopping," which is to leave the board at this point, returning and hitting it for the takeoff instead of pressing it.

Arm swing faults

a. forward bend, arms back

b. weight back before spring

c. "crow-hop"

The critical point of the takeoff is the press itself, this being the resultant force imparted to the board for the spring. The problem here is an accurate sense of timing, correct degree of flexion, control of balance and alignment, and a finish with strong extension.

The procedure for the standard back arm swing and body mechanics should be drilled on the side of the pool to the point where it is easy and unhesitating. Check students for smoothness, for coordination into a vertical spring, and for alignment. The teacher can help physically by standing behind the student and moving with him, forcing the correct position and timing.

Arm swing practice on land

D. COMPLETE BACK DIVE

In putting this pattern together on the board the beginner is likely to concentrate solely on the successive steps for the takeoff and to forget completely that the whole thing finishes with him in midair. At this point many novices freeze, and land resoundingly on their backs. It is important after the land drill to point out that the action *following* the takeoff press and extension is the same as for the beginning back spring: arms up, over and back; head lifts up and back with the arms; look for the water—you're in.

For the first try with the complete takeoff, stress smoothness, balance, and an easy extension. Play the dive for control and understanding, not initially for height. The slight lean which was a part of the initial back spring should not be mentioned now. The direction normally taken by the arms in the swing, plus the beginner's anticipation in head action, is enough to take the body outward. The very occasional time that a beginner comes too close is caused by an incomplete takeoff push, which is discussed on page 90.

Any large errors in these first back dives will be quite easy to see and to correct. Some may over-anticipate the dive and lean back enough on the takeoff to overthrow badly; or the lean may give them great distance. Some may freeze psychologically (and physically) and all sorts of strange incorrect actions may then occur. Most of the obvious faults have obvious corrections. It is a question of communicating the understanding of the cause of the fault to the student—by image, by kinesthetic awareness, by overcorrection, by pointing out similar errors in other students. Over-tenseness, great fear, or inhibition mean that the progression has been a bit fast for the individual, and he needs to go back a stage or two and spend more time working up to the dive again. On the other hand this kind of yielding to the preference of the student can sometimes be the worst thing to. This student may *need* to be dared, pushed, forced into doing the more advanced thing—not be allowed to hide behind higher and higher barriers of reluctance and timidity. Acute perception is needed to judge the temperament of the student and to decide what is the best course of action.

E. BACK DIVE MECHANICS

1) Hip Lift

Immediately following the arm lift and body extension, but before leaving the board, the diver must add hip lift,[6] easing the head back, and then guide the dive into the water. The hip lift must be started strongly and at the split second following the leg push. This hip lift is really a reverse hip lift, as we think of it in a front dive or front jack knife. It is a strong press from behind, the feeling of pushing one's hip bones toward the ceiling. In muscle action, it is a strong contraction of the glutei and abdominal muscles, much akin to pelvic contraction in modern dance technique. The result is a rotation with height, utilizing and continuing the rise begun with the takeoff.

[6] Technically, the hip lift is started as the diver leaves the board but is still in contact with it. However, if divers are conscious of this, they tend to press the hips into action too soon. The diver's *feeling* is that it occurs just after leaving the board.

If the hip lift is started too early, the diver will "cut back"—will actually push his center of gravity slightly forward over the board. This will bring him very close to the board just as it did for the forward takeoff. It will also cut off his height since he will not have made use of the full spring, either of the board or of his own legs.

Back dive "cut back"

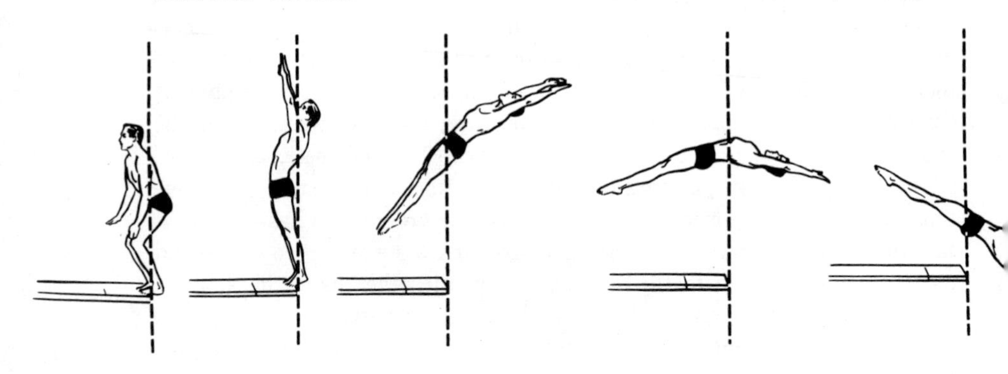

Too much arch, flat landing

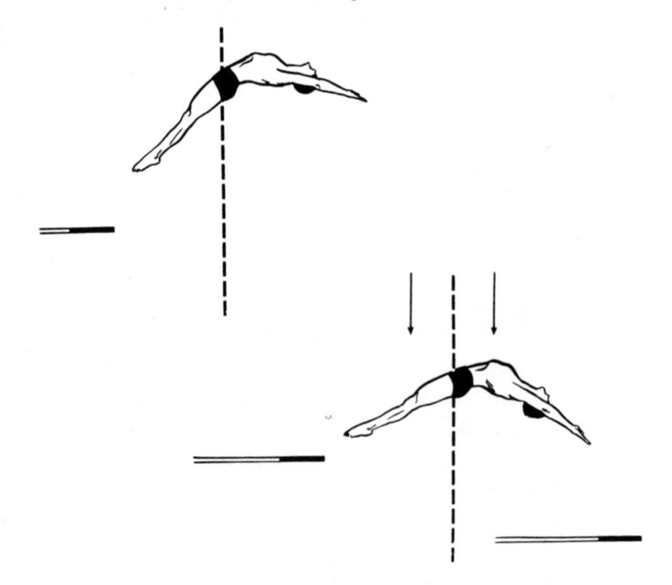

Beginning back divers, especially girls, often have the notion that a good back dive is done with as much back bend as possible. This notion has led to many red backs. A deep arch, meaning a lower back (or lumbar) arch, keeps the hip position set as it is on leaving the board, while the upper body bends back. So the feet remain stationary (do not rotate) and the body hangs, entering the water head and feet simultaneously. *Upper* back extension should be present, but any degree of *lower* back arch will inhibit hip lift and rotation.

The strong hip lift should be started during the takeoff, and only started. This is enough for a mere half rotation, which the back dive is. Too much strength and speed of rotation will carry the diver right on over to his stomach. He should turn only enough to see the water at the peak of the dive, then guide back for his entry accordingly.

The hip lift, coordinated with correct takeoff spring, is the key to height in the back dive. The same hip action is used for reverse dives ("half gainers"), and even more strongly for back somersaults in the layout position. It can be felt and sometimes best understood as an exercise on the side of the pool:

Standing, pelvic contraction

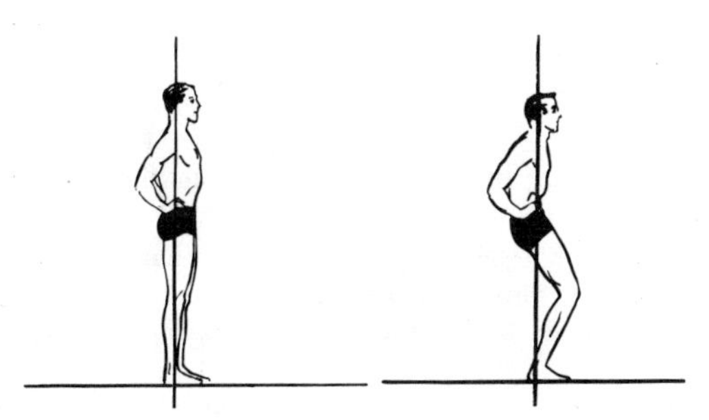

"Long" jump from side of pool

It can also be practiced in the form of a jump from the side of the pool. Be sure that the jump is taken well away from the wall to avoid any chance of hitting the side. In the execution of the hip rotation there should be no arch at all, and no hip flexion.

2) Arm Action

Leaving the board the arms reach upward in an arc backward. "Pull" effort must be regulated by the speed of rotation as dictated by a combination of leg push on the board, hip lift, and head control.

For the beginner the arms are best used in parallel. As he masters the dive he should then advance to the open position of the arms, called by the youngsters a back swan. The advantages of the open position are increased control of the dive and esthetically a more graceful line.

Arm positions in flight

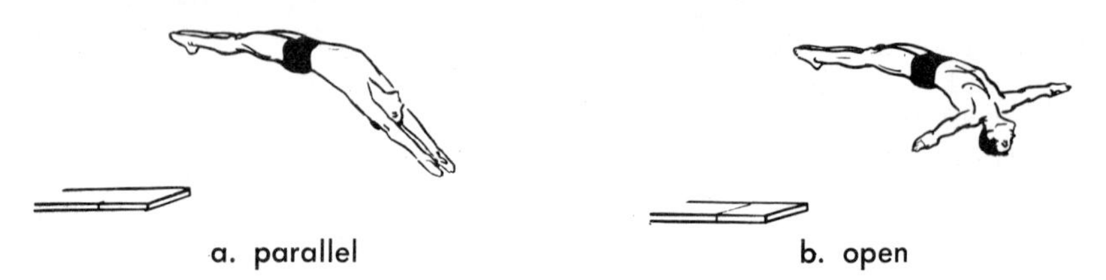

a. parallel b. open

The justification for the initial parallel arm position is three-fold:

a) It carries on what has been the arm position for the steps leading up to the back dive, thus eliminating a new factor of concentration.
b) It allows the diver to feel the whereabouts and the tension of the rest of his body better.
c) It eliminates faults in the open position which seem to be inevitable when it is used before the back dive is really "set."

Faults in arm position

The open position is executed by first reaching upward, then opening into a horizontal position with palms up. The arms should be as nearly at ninety degrees to the body as possible. As the body turns, arm tension and outward or inward rotation at the shoulder joint can be used as rotational controlling factors. They should be held in position as long as possible. When closing in for the back entry they are important in controlling entry angle.

Arm action

a. attempting to save short dive b. attempting to save dive going over

3) Head Action

The head is in line with the body on takeoff press. Even in the final extension from the board the diver should feel that he is pushing through the top of his head. Once in the air, the head should ride back smoothly with a lift of the chin and the back of the neck held fairly firm. The head should move in line with the general rotation of the dive. It is always in a position of control to allow quick adjustments.

4) Timing

"Timing" is an elusive thing for the diver. It starts with preferred speed of spring into takeoff; involves how much effort is to be put into what has to be done, and how long that effort is to be continued. In the back dive, a rotation of 180 degrees, the force and effort should carry the diver to a half rotation (90 degrees) by the time maximum height is reached. Then, in the logical arc of the dive, the fall can be used to guide the dive in easily for the entry. If the diver is *not* just "over the top" at the top, he will be fighting all the way down to accomplish the rest of the rotation. On the other hand, if he is a shade too far in his rotation at the peak of the dive, he will be unable to control his fall, or to "check" his dive, and will sail on beyond and over.

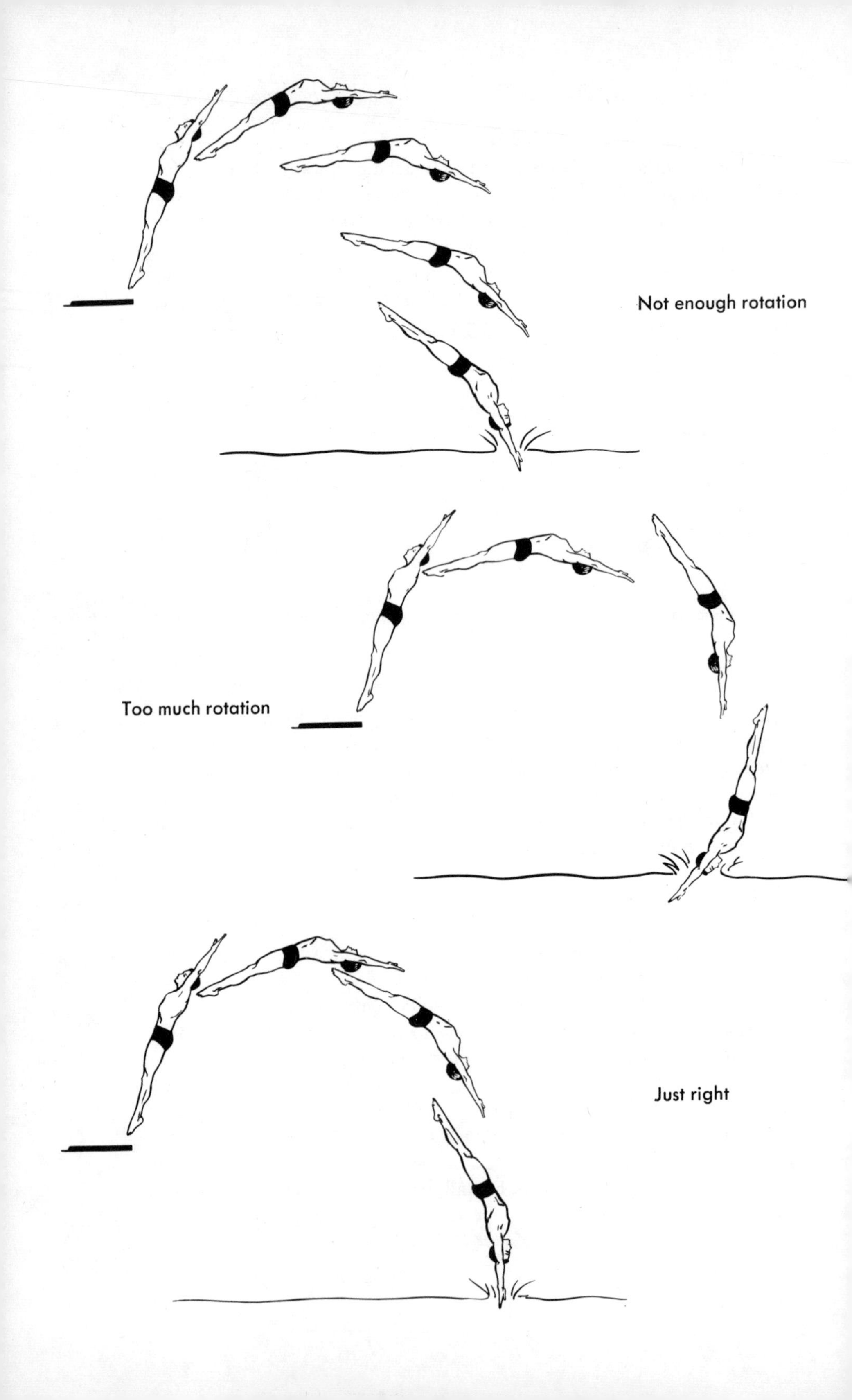
Not enough rotation
Too much rotation
Just right

Any errors along the way will spoil the timing—a lean from the board, lack of height, too little hip lift, too much hip lift, incorrect head action one way or another, arm and shoulder pull out of line and many, many other possible imbalances. Student and teacher should work together to find the mistakes and to correct the imbalances. In the end, with the takeoff and mechanics good, it still comes back to a *feeling*—different from person to person—of just how much effort accomplishes just how much for each diver.

5) Entry

The back dive entry (from the layout position) has a slight arch so that the direction of rotation is continued under water. This arch and rotation is very small. The entry angle is, as in the front dive, short of the vertical.

Good entry

An entry which is really ninety degrees will make it hard for the diver to keep from toppling over or dropping his legs into a pike. A deep arch with the entry point beneath him will cause a scoop entry with the legs going over.

Back dive entry faults

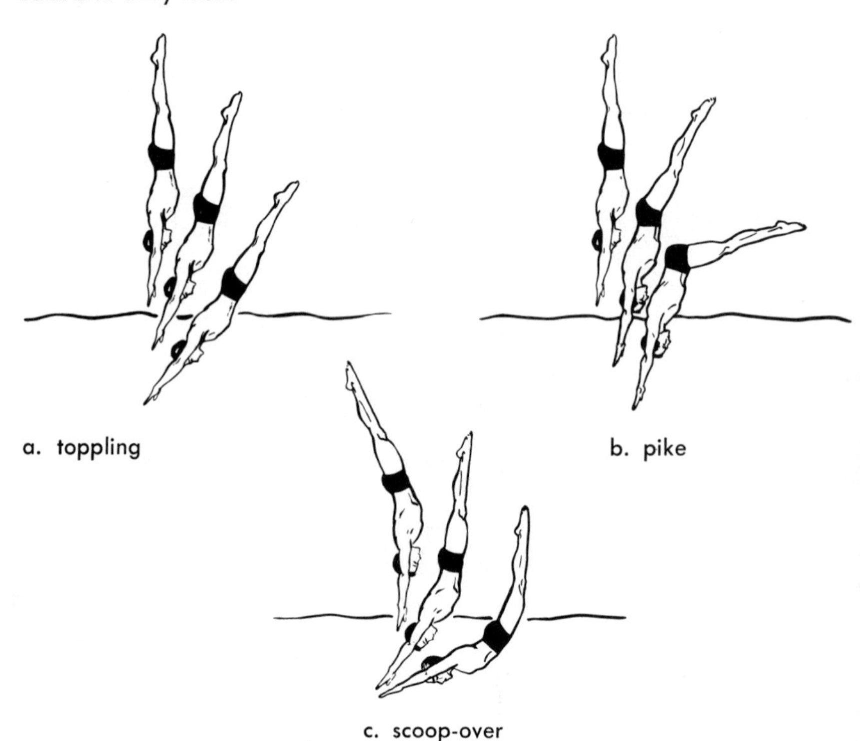

a. toppling

b. pike

c. scoop-over

How does the diver plan for his back entry? He should see the water below between his arms as they are closing for entry. Then he should stretch the arms harder as they near the water, his hands coming together a few inches above the surface. Along with the arm and shoulder stretch, he tucks his chin, stretches the back of his neck and his whole spine in a straight line, removing most of the thoracic arch needed in the execution of the dive.

The procedure for the back entry should be followed for all dives having the identical entry direction; that is, back one-and-a-half somersault, half twist, reverse dive, reverse one-and-a-half somersault.

10

General Progression

A. WHAT LIES AHEAD

Having accomplished the initial thing, the "getting in head first," let's consider the scope of what lies ahead. Names of dives appear complicated and ominous to the uninitiated. The lay spectator is impressed, as always, by that which he does not understand. In addition, there is the problem that the youngster learning may be reluctant to leave his comfortable "head first" plateau.

These are the bare facts: all dives are either forward or backward. These are the only two directions in which a diver can go. One can add a "twist," but this is *added* to the forward or backward direction, thus is not an independent rotation. The rest of the complication and/or confusion is a matter of whether the diver starts out walking straight off the board, whether he seems to change his mind and turn over backward toward the board after leaving it, or whether he may start out standing with his back to the water. He himself can only turn in a forward or backward direction. He may cloud the issue by assuming different positions in the process of his rotation such as doubling up, or touching his toes.

Here is a more technical outline of the diving groups (which means the specific direction of rotation):

1. *Forward Group:* diver takes forward approach, rotates forward around a horizontal axis. Includes front dive (swan dive, front jackknife), forward somersault, forward one-and-a-half somersault, etc.
2. *Backward Group:* diver starts with his back to the water; rotates backward around a horizontal axis. Includes back dive, back dive, back somersault, back one-and-a-half somersault, etc.

Front dive

Back dive

3. *Reverse Group* (formerly Gainer Group): diver takes forward approach; just after takeoff, rotates backward (toward the board) on a horizontal axis. Includes reverse dive (half gainer), reverse somersault (full gainer), reverse one-and-a-half somersault, etc.
4. *Inward Group* (formerly Cutaway Group): diver starts with his back to the water; just after takeoff, rotates forward (toward the board) around a horizontal axis. Includes inward dive (back jackknife, cutaway swan), inward somersault (cutaway somersault), inward one-and-a-half somersault, etc.

Reverse dive

Inward dive

5. *Twisting Group:* any dive in which a rotation around the body's vertical axis is added to the normal rotation of the dive. Includes half twist, full twist, forward somersault with full twist, back dive with half twist, reverse dive with half twist, etc.

Half twist

So much for direction *per se*. The diver can, while rotating forward or backward, assume one of three basic positions. In fact he can, upon occasion, go from one position to another within the same dive. The three basic positions are:

1. (a[7]) *Layout:* body extended; arms either parallel overhead or in

[7] In all competitive rulebooks the positions are known as "a," "b," and "c" as designated above. For example, a reverse dive in the pike position is listed as a reverse dive "b"; a swan dive as a front dive "a."

a side horizontal (swan) position. Back may have some degree of arch.

Layout positions

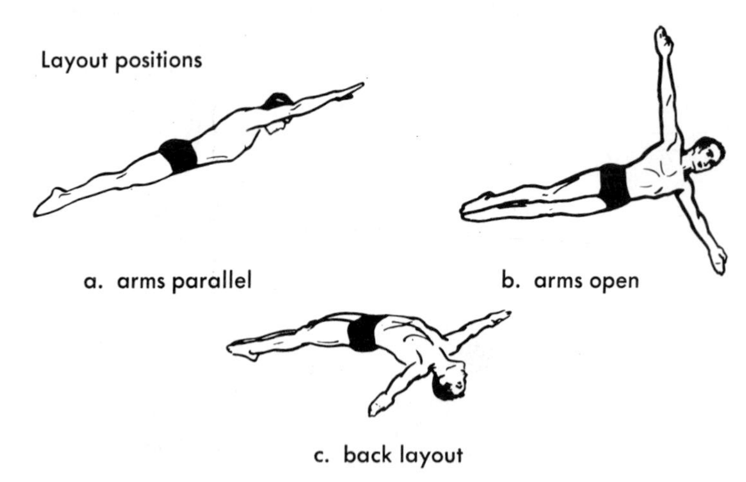

a. arms parallel

b. arms open

c. back layout

2\. (b) *Pike:* body flexed at the hips, knees straight. In form dives, hands at ankles. In spinning dives, hand behind knees (closed pike) or extended to the side (open pike).

Pike positions

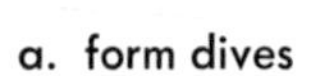

a. form dives

b. closed pike

c. open pike

3\. (c) *Tuck:* body flexed at spine, hips, and knees, with hands at ankles—colloquially, "rolled up in a ball."

Tuck position

The positions allow for a change of pace in air speed: tuck spins are more compact than pike spins and therefore are faster.[8] The layout position makes for a longer, more graceful line, as desired for a swan dive or a half twist. Facility in all the positions gives diving more variety and gives the divers a seemingly greater repertoire. In addition, the positions allow for individual differences in body structure. Many look better in the pike position than in the tuck position, and can capitalize on this in choosing dives for competition or exhibition.

Changes of position within one dive are used mostly in what are called "flying" dives. This is when a layout with a good deal of rotational speed is started, followed by a collapse in the same direction into a pike or tuck spin.

Flying back somersault

This has quite a surprise element because of the sharp contrast in the speed of a layout rotation and of a pike or tuck rotation. It is a similar sensation to figure skating spins, when the skater brings his arms in sharply from an open arm position and you see the spin accelerate.

---

[8] See p. 16

B. DEGREE OF DIFFICULTY

Every official dive is listed in competitive rule books with a "degree of difficulty": a numerical rating assigned to that dive according to its ease or difficulty of performance. The ratings are graded with reference to the position of the dive (tuck, pike, or layout) and to the height of the board from the water (one or three meters). A forward dive pike (jackknife) is rated 1.4 from the one meter board, 1.5 from the three meter; a reverse dive layout (half gainer) is 1.8 and 1.9. On the one meter, a forward one-and-a-half in tuck position is 1.6; in pike is 1.7.

These degrees of difficulty are important only in relation to competitive diving where they are multiplied by the judges' scores. This means that a dive is judged on performance alone, not on how hard it is. The degree of difficulty table represents an effort to make diving judging as objective as possible.

C. WHAT TO TEACH NEXT

The question of the proper order of teaching specific dives arises about now. The plain front and back dives should be the initial dives as the foundation for the only two directions in which one can revolve (except for the addition of twists). These two can be worked on simultaneously, since neither depends in any way upon the other.

Following the front and back dives, experts differ, often with parallel success. The order of learning is only a part of the picture. Different teachers and different individual divers may vary greatly in progression, and all achieve excellent results.

My personal order of teaching follows. Even this will vary with me at different times, and so I do not feel that the beginning teacher should take this progression as gospel, but perhaps as a point of departure. The essential principle is that there should be a logical sequence from the known to the unknown, from one related movement to another without too wide a gap between the old and the new.

Suggested Progression

1. Front dive.
2. Back dive.
3. Front jackknife.

This is the easiest of all dives. The hip flexion involved is a natural action; the control and force of this flexion is the basis of good hip lift for forward spins.

4. Back somersault (tuck).
   This is usually best for the first type of spin, although occasionally difficult for those who have a psychological block about going backward. The takeoff balance is simple from the stationary position. The beginner is soon at home in the turn, as he can see the water almost from the start.
5. Forward somersault (tuck).
   Here the hip lift learned in the front jackknife is applied. The timing of the turn is more difficult than for the back somersault since the entry point cannot be seen.
6. Half twist.
   The experience of both front and back dives is necessary. Now we add more complex mechanics for adding rotation on a longitudinal axis.
7. Inward dive (pike) formerly, Back jackknife.
   This is an adaptation of the front jackknife hip lift. It gives a new feeling because the lift is initiated from a back takeoff start.
8. Swan dive (front dive with new arm position).
   While the mechanics are simple, they are very difficult to master. The swan could be placed earlier in the progression, but is seldom successful until the diver has really consistent boardwork and considerable diving experience.

These eight represent basic dives from each of four of the five diving groups,[9] and the order of what follows after these is not too vital. As far as the teaching of the basic dives goes, the two chapters following are concerned with the details of each of the six dives not yet discussed in detail.

In terms of progression, the beginning teacher may want to know how to tell *when* to progress to the next dive on the list. When is the student "ready" for the next step? This kind of judgment comes with teaching experience. The diver must have a fair degree of consistency, confidence, and success in the preceding step of the progression, and a desire to move along himself. One's standards vary, but safety, and reasonable confidence in the teacher's mind that the student has the potential for this next step, are the two primary factors. Where dives have no real relationship to each

[9] The group omitted, the reverse (gainer) group, is discussed in Chapter 13.

other, such as a back somersault and a half twist, the student most certainly can be learning both in the same practice periods. We cannot hold out for perfection to the point of stifling all incentive to try new things. The good teacher maintains a balance between working on the familiar dives now easily accomplished and adding new material or new slants in emphasis to correct old problems.

The material in the following two chapters is organized in the following manner for each dive:

Must Know Already:

This is a statement of what learning is essential before the new dive is attempted.

Initial Instructions:

These are the basic instructions which you, the teacher, may tell the student for his first try. These instructions are deliberately and deceptively simple, as they *must* be in order to make the essential action clear and comprehensive to the student.

Details and Coaching Points:

Justification and background for the preceding "initial instruction;" the whys and wherefores for the teacher and for the students' questions and understanding as he progresses.

Common Faults and General Corrections:

These will sometimes be listed separately and sometimes discussed together.

Specific listing of faults and corrections in a table form has been avoided since there is almost always overlapping of cause and effect. There is rarely a single cause for any fault and rarely an absolute correction without necessary consideration of several possible influences. A table listing of faults and corrections can therefore be greatly misleading.

II

Basic Dives A

1. FRONT JACKKNIFE [10]

Must Know Already:

Forward approach and plain front dive to a degree of fair consistency.

Initial Instructions:

Take your usual approach. At the takeoff, try to leave your feet where they are (underneath you). Bend over and touch your ankles quickly before your legs have a chance to go back. Keep looking at the water and dive in straight.

Details and Coaching Points:

The student has had no experience except straight front dives. Thus every forward takeoff has been followed by an arc, the legs following the line of this arc from the start. Now we want his feet to remain in a vertical position while the body folds in the middle. This factor of holding the leg line vertical is the first new feeling to teach.

---

[10] The term "jackknife" is peculiarly American. Technically it is a forward dive in pike, or "b," position. We shall call it a jackknife throughout since this is the familiar name.

Front dive with jackknife superimposed

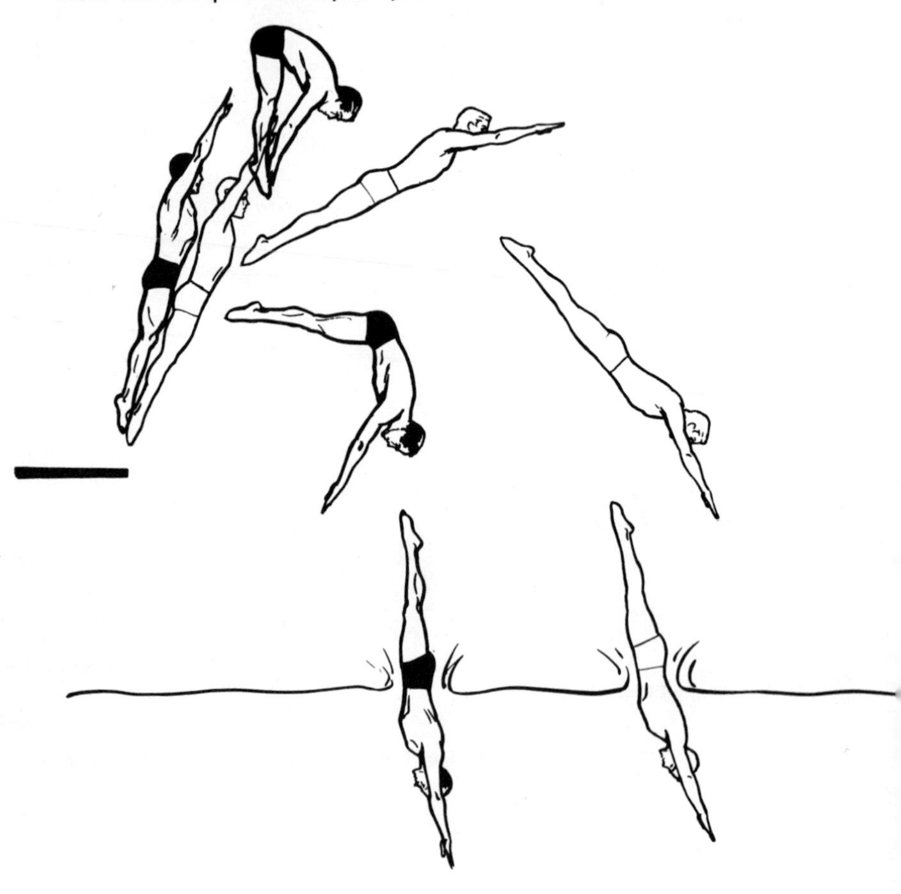

If the feeling of holding the legs straight down is not mentioned, the beginner will most likely let his legs go back as usual, will try to reach his ankles without bending, and will complain that he "cannot touch his toes."

Pike attempt, legs too far back

An explanation which sometimes reaches the beginner is this: that a jackknife is a straight dive done in two parts. First the upper part of the body bends over, the legs doing nothing. Then the lower part of the body comes up behind while the head and arms are held stable.

The pike is really accomplished by a strong abdominal contraction against the stabilizing action of the leg muscles which act as fixators. This jackknife or pike action is often called "hip lift," and as such has a part in the beginning of many dives. Yet the "hips" do not accomplish the action; the abdominal muscles *do*. After a few attempts following the simple initial instructions, even the beginner should be made to understand this basic action of the pike. Coaching points such as to "suck in" help; or to pretend that someone has punched you in the middle; or a visualization of the diver as a puppet, and a string attached to the tail bone is pulled sharply upward.

A useful exercise for the pike lift is to place the hands on the side of the lowboard, jump and take the weight on the hands, pulling the hips as high over the shoulders as possible. Note that the legs must be strongly held not to swing back. The head is "out" of the dive; that is, neither ducked nor lifted, but watching the water from the peak of the hip bend,

Pike exercise

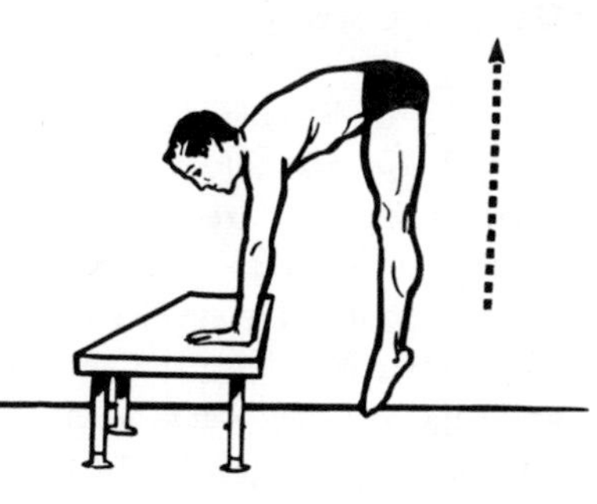

looking straight down over the insteps. Thus the position of the head is controlled by the focus of the eyes on the water below.

The hands may be placed on the ankles or insteps, or may grasp ankles or insteps. The requirement of the dive is flexion at the hip joint with the knees straight, and contact with the hands at the feet.

From the peak of the dive to the entry, the diver should aim and stretch the upper part of the body to the water. His legs should ride back under control to the vertical. At first one's instinct is to kick back, or at least press back, with the legs. The balance at the top should be such that the legs will go back almost by themselves with a weightless feeling. In fact, the feeling of heaviness or of extreme lightness in the legs is a major clue by which an advanced diver can judge his error in position, and can act accordingly to adjust his entry spot to "save" the dive.

As the student becomes more expert, he should begin to be conscious of the arm lift at the beginning into the pike and must emphasize this if he wants to gain more height in the dive. It must be done quickly, since he should be in the pike position at the peak of the dive.

Common Faults:

The beginner's faults will be very obvious: not holding the legs down in the pike, thus swinging over or not reaching a pike position at all; lack of hip lift from the start; not using any arm lift at the start; ducking the head in the pike and rolling over blindly; pushing feet forward at the start and landing very shallow; form faults of knee bendings, legs apart and poor foot position; kicking out of the pike and on over; spoiling good drops into the entry by not watching and aiming; not aligning the arms with the body on the drop; or swinging from the pike position into an arch at the entry.

General Corrections:

a) An understanding of the dive mechanics: check that the students really know and understand what they are trying to do and also realize what faults they are committing. If a long mirror is available let them check their own pike positions on land.

b) Practice pike surface dives for the feeling of the hip lift and for the proper extension into the vertical position. Correct body alignment of the students. Do they *know* when their hips are no longer in flexion but have not yet over-extended into an arch? It's the familiar correction for all entries: a checking of motion with the abdominal muscles and firm alignment of the whole spine.

2. BACK SOMERSAULT (tuck)

Must Know Already:

The back dive, for the takeoff spring in that direction, and general backward rotation.

Initial Instructions:

Do a normal back takeoff spring. Directly following the press on the board, flex knees sharply to your chest. Pull on the shins, look for the water; let go, or else hold the tuck position and "cannonball" in. The head does not go hard back on the turn. Concentrate on a good spring followed by strong knee action—this will turn you easily. (If the student has a safe back spring with the proper distance into his back dive, the teacher need not stress distance. You know your own students: if the takeoff is inconsistent or shows tendencies to cut in close, then a little coaching for lean may be advisable.)

Details and Coaching Points:

There are no progressive steps into a back somersault. It does help some beginners to do a few on the surface of the water for the feel of complete backward revolution. And one can practice the initial knee and upper back action, one leg at a time, while standing on the pool deck. The simple instructions above are all that are needed for the first attempts. It will not take much to turn the diver over, even if the tuck is not held at first. Occasionally the student will turn very little, taking some back slaps. This is usually caused by great inhibition and resistance to rolling over backward, and indicates a need for much practice on somersaults on the surface of the water.

Be careful not to say too much about the "break" on the first few dives. The novice will frequently anticipate the break. In the general confusion and dizziness of the first try, he may think that he has turned farther than he really has, and end up horizontally. In his first few tries he should *feel* the turn, which means he should try to be aware of when he is upside down and when he is rightside up. Then he can begin to look for the water beneath him as he comes rightside up, and try letting go to stand up.

The diver should try for the correct tuck position before very long so that he will not form the habit of a sloppy position. The tuck is the most compact of the spinning positions, and is therefore the easiest in which to rotate. Whether the tuck spin is in a forward or a backward direction, the exact position varies only slightly in head and spinal alignment. Hands should be grasped around the shins (one hand to each leg) at a point between ankles and knees which will keep the tuck tightest for that individual. Elbows should be close to the sides, toes pointed, knees close to chest, heels close to buttocks. Students may try it on the side, one leg at a time, or sit on the floor and experiment with the position, or perhaps try it on the surface of the water.

Tuck position practice

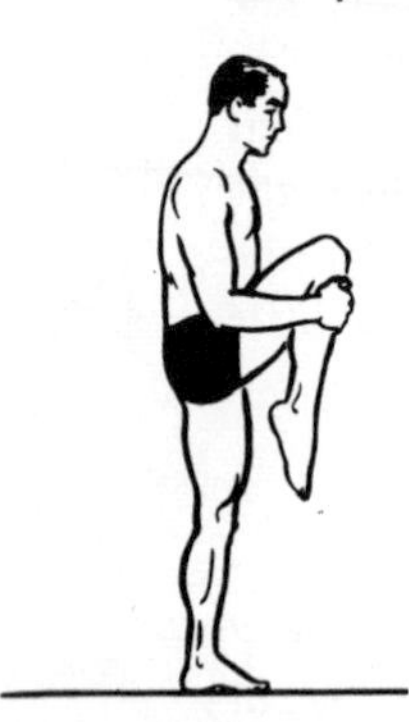

a. standing on one leg

b. squatting on floor

c. elbows out: wrong

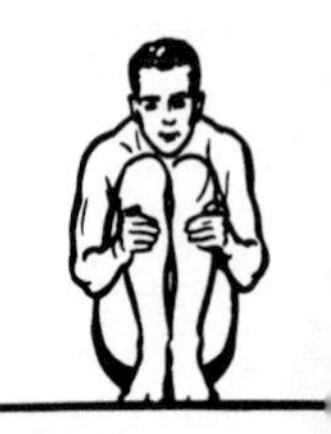

d. correct elbow position

For a back somersault, the head is more in line with the spine and the spine more erect than for the forward spins.

a. forward tuck

b. backward tuck

Two points should be made clear very early: first, that the knees must be brought *to* the hands, and secondly, that the head is *not* thrown back at all, but pressed back in line with the neck and upper spine. This press will be felt in the back of the neck and in the upper back between the shoulder blades.

Eventually the diver learns to use arm lift into the somersault. At first he tends to fold up into the tuck, in which case he actually lowers his arms after takeoff. As more height is obtained and the spin is faster, the arm reach should be emphasized, the knees coming into the hands, the body thus rotating to meet the hands.

Initiating spin

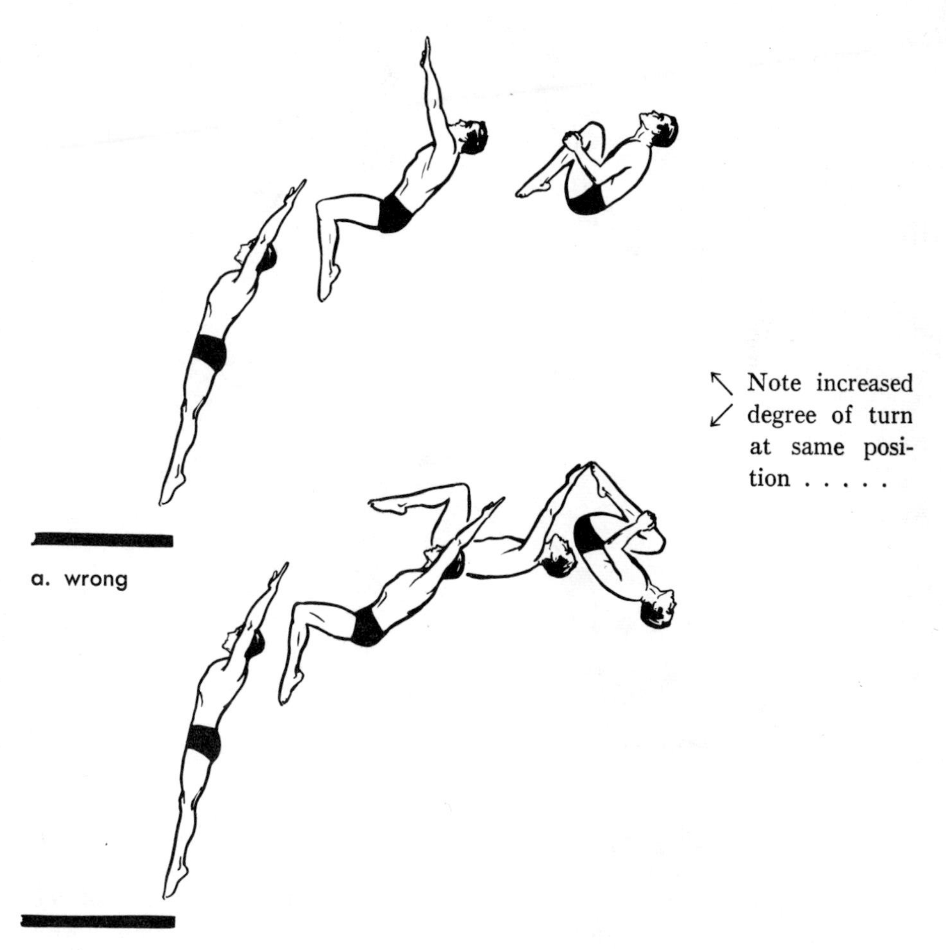

Thus by the time the tuck is actually assumed (that is, contact made), the rotation is half done!

The particular feeling of pressing back the head and neck in a back spin has to be consciously practiced. Instinctively the diver wants to lift his chin and pull back with the head. This makes it very difficult to get into the tuck and tends to make the diver cut off his height in his anxiety to go back.

Head action in back spin

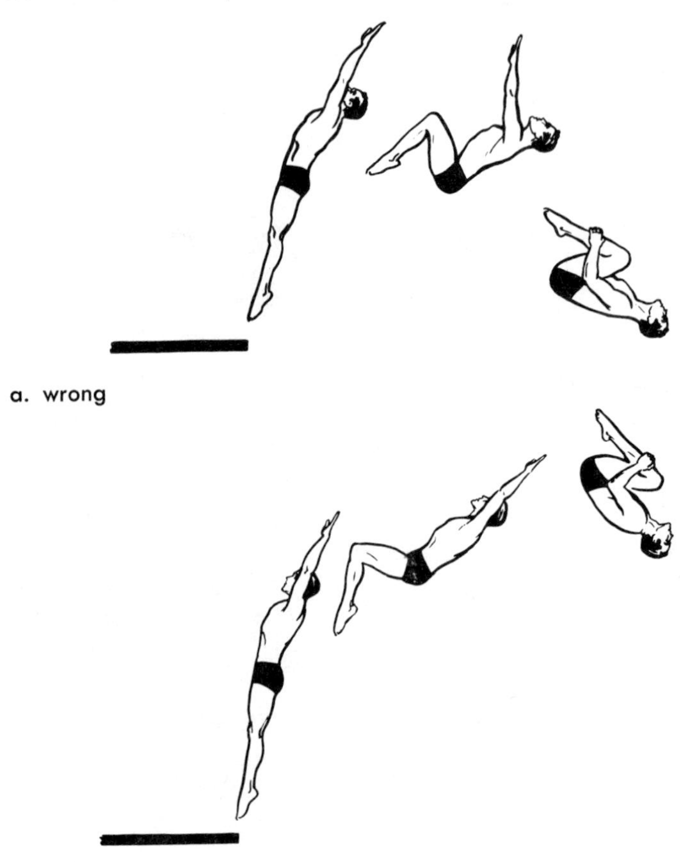

a. wrong

b. right

The fine points of gaining height in the back somersault have to do with the exact timing of the knee lift in relation to the rise of the body from the board, and with the guiding of the head with the line of force of the spring. All of these are sensitivities the diver must work out himself, with the help of the teacher as an observer. Another factor in height, and in the power and speed of the spin, is the muscular force from the board into the spin. This is accomplished by abdominal contraction against a fixed lower back, so that the tuck is not a folding or collapsing, but a powerful driving rotation. The difference between a dead lifeless roll and an exciting forceful spin is this combination of muscular effort, timing, and balance.

The break from the tuck into the extended position and entry begins as the diver sees the water below and judges his rotation in relation to it. As his speed of spin may vary slightly from dive to dive (as will his height, allowing for differences in boards), he will have to look for and judge his entry on each and every dive. He must break with definiteness, neither leisurely nor jerkily, and must plan to be extended for entry slightly before he reaches the vertical.

Common Faults and General Corrections:

Some faults have been discussed in the process of explaining the mechanics of the back spin, such as not bringing up the knees, lack of arm lift and maintenance of the upward stretch of the arms, head and neck action faults, and omission of a positive abdominal contraction. These mechanics have mostly to do with the success of the spin itself. Failure to do them correctly results in sluggish spins, with very hard work to make it around to a foot first entry.

Going back to general faults from the beginning: a lean back on the takeoff will give more speed to the spin, but often takes it out of control. If nothing else, a lean of any degree will make the arc of the dive low and far out. A pickup of the knees too early in the takeoff mechanics (cut back) will bring the diver close to the board:

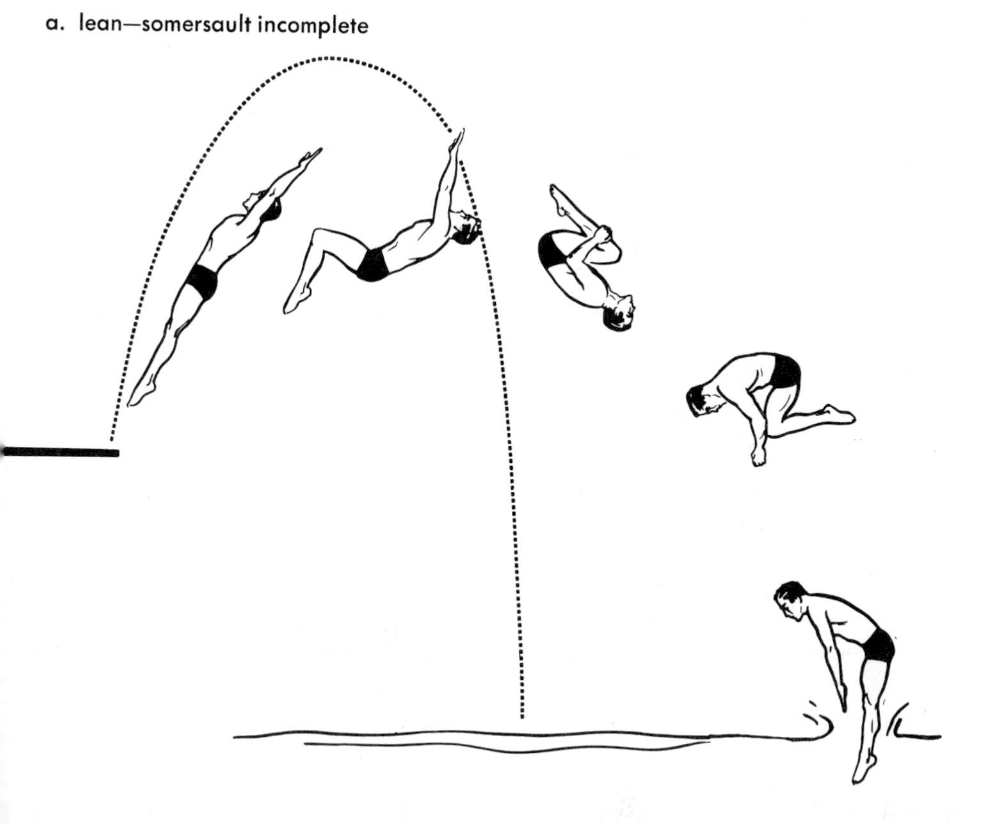

b. "cut back"

If either of these takeoff faults is present, practice for a stable consistent back jump is indicated.

Common faults in the tuck position are failure to fold up tightly; hand position too low toward ankles, making the diver pull his knees away from his chest; or, conversely, hands placed too close to the knees, which makes the heels swing out away from the buttocks, and sometimes causes the hands to skid right off the knees.

In the break, slowness may make the diver tend to ride into a pike and scoop into the water: a sudden jerky break often checks the drop too hard, and the entry is shallow. A late break carries him right on over.

Watch for the diver's alignment on the entry. The total line may be correct, but relaxed abdominals will allow an arch. The head must be brought into line after having been focused downward at the water. The toes must remain pointed.

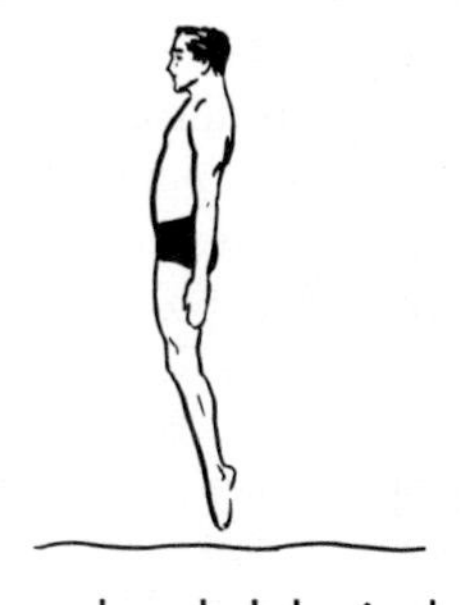

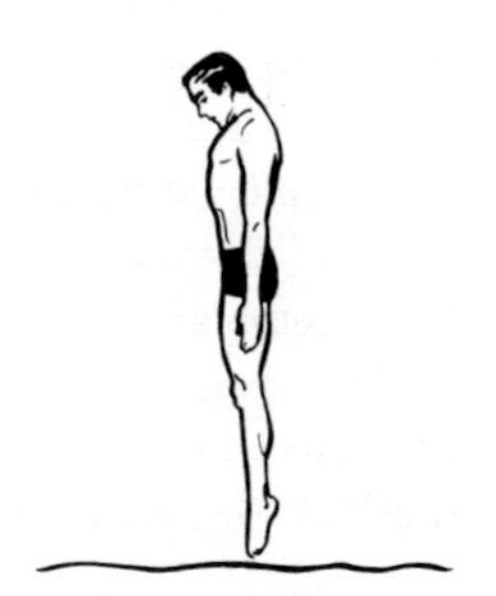

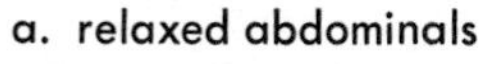

a. relaxed abdominals

b. the forgotten head

3. FORWARD SOMERSAULT (tuck)

Must Know Already:

Plain front dive to a point of reasonable boardwork and consistent take-off. The front jackknife is advisable for experience in hip lift. *Note*: A forward somersault is best taught in a series of progressive steps rather than attempted without preamble as in the back somersault.

A) ROLL-IN FROM SIDE

Initial Instructions:

From the side of the pool or dock, squat and assume the tuck position, duck head, roll in.

Roll-in

Details and Coaching Points:

The tuck should be held snugly, one hand on each shin halfway between the ankle and the knee. On rolling in, the balance should be directed well out from the side to avoid any chance of hitting the side. The tuck should be tightly maintained into the water—no loosening of position at all. Here at the start of learning the somersault and all the way through, there should be no countenancing of the do-it-yourself swimmin' hole type of "flip," in which the youngster just throws himself over and around with no semblance of form. The correct tuck position should be stressed from the beginning, not only for looks, but also because the student will then learn the proper spin mechanics.

Watch especially the head position: chin in, head well down even at the entry.

B) SPIN FROM HALF-ERECT POSITION (SIDE)

Initial Instructions:

Stand on the side, semi-flexed position, arms forward. Lean, throw head and arms down into tuck position, spin into the water.

Spin from semi-flexed position

Details and Coaching Points:

The first step was a rolling in, learning the position of the forward tuck, the feel of turning over and maintaining the tuck. Now we have added a more vertical start, a "throw" into the tuck. This throw will involve pushing with the legs, but the emphasis at first should be on the head-arm-shoulder action down into the tuck. The lean will assure safe distance and also will impart more rotation. The spin will be low but fast, and done properly, will carry most students slightly over.

If the spin at this stage carries the student over to a considerable degree so that he is getting face slaps, the next step (c) should be tried right away. If the spin is faulty and slow, or the beginner is not maintaining the tuck and breaking flat (on his back), keep working at this stage. *But,* do not keep pounding on this one too long on the same day when the student is hitting badly. He will become really bruised and will be set back psychologically. Rather switch to something quite different and make a fresh start on spins another day.

Bringing knees to hands (fault)

Here in step (b) the student begins to learn the principles of the forward spin. The diver must really go after his shins with his hands, avoid bringing them up at all, in forming his tuck. This means that he is actually upside down when the tuck position is reached (as in the back somersault).

C) SPIN FROM ERECT POSITION (SIDE)

Initial Instructions:

Stand straight on the side. Lean and throw into the somersault. Try now to feel the leg push more strongly, along with a fast, hard hip lift at the same time as the arms throw down into the tuck. Begin to be conscious of when you are upside down and when you are again right side up. Try to make the initial action of the arms reach higher over an arc into the tuck.

Details and Coaching Points:

Stress importance of spring-hip lift coordination into the spins. When the spin seems good, consistently over, and the student has an awareness of when he is upside down and right side up, then he can try letting go when he feels he has completed the turn. This should be just the start of a break. It is common to anticipate this, to break early and flat, so the idea of the break is deliberately left until late in the progression.

In a front somersault it is very hard to have any focal point for knowing *when* to break. One can look for something straight ahead or slightly above. If you spot the water below, it will carry you too far around. If you do much "looking" during any spin, you find a confusion of walls or trees or people whizzing by. So the real clue is this awareness of upside down and right side up—actually a balance perception in the middle ear. Some call it "timing." At any rate, it is an inner physical knowledge of one revolution, not based on any visual relationship. The eyes, however, should not be closed. They should be open, but not consciously focusing. Let the confusion slide by; concentrate on the physical mechanics of the spin. Only become aware of what you are seeing at the very end as you slide into the water.

Now the student should be ready for the board. He knows that he can turn over and come to a standing position with a takeoff from a non-flexible surface and from a height of eighteen inches at the most. There are some who feel at this point the student should take an approach to try his first somersault from the board. I feel that the student should try a standing somersault from the end of the board much the same as step (c) from the side of the pool.

D) STANDING ON THE BOARD

Initial Instructions:

Stand on the end of the board, arms in front, elbows slightly flexed. Bend knees slightly and push; lift hips hard; throw into tuck. Ease out and stand up when you feel you have completed the turn.

Starting position for standing forward somersault

Details and Coaching Points:

Lean need not be mentioned usually. The starting position of the arms, plus the direction of rotation, plus the beginner's general tendency to lean anyway, take care of the safety angle. Very occasionally, you may have noted an individual who is apt to cut back in his spin from the side—to pick up his hips a little too straight. For this particular individual, you might feel it necessary to coach a slight lean.

Basically, this somersault should be much easier from the springboard. It is a softer feeling of hip lift with the flexibility of the board now helping out. Yet the initial hip lift must be done just as forcefully and sharply as from the hard tile of the poolside. Only *after* the lift and rotation have been started can the diver ease up and guide his way more leisurely into the water. If that initial lift is not strong, is lazier and slower than from the side, the spin will never get started at all, no matter how hard one works for it in the air.

Common Faults and General Corrections:

The problems one expects on the initial standing forward somersault from the board are about as follows:

1) those who think they will turn much faster now, and anticipate the break—flat on their backs.

2) those who follow directions literally (rare!) and put exactly the same hard effort and lift force into this first try on the board, go beyond the single turn to land flat on their faces. (Sometimes an extreme lean on the takeoff will cause a fast, wild spin which is out of control.)
3) those who "black out" en route, and anything can happen, although they don't know where they are until they hit the water.
4) the lucky ones who do everything just right and drop in correctly for a single turn. This will happen sometimes on a first try—pure luck with no particular planning behind it. Be prepared for subsequent timing troubles which are all the more discouraging because of early successes.

On the whole the ones who have developed a good consistent spin from the side will not have much trouble. When students *do* have much difficulty, they should go right back to the side for more practice and confidence.

This "blacking out" business should be explained. It seems to be a building up of fear and uncertainty to a point where the mind is no longer aware of the body's position in space or length of time in space. The sensation is that one leaves the board, is overwhelmed by a turning-falling sensation without control or volition, as in a dream. The rude awakening comes when the water is hit—and one doesn't have any idea whether this will be on head, feet, side, back, or face.

There is rarely a beginner, that is, one attempting any new dive for the first time, who does not have a few "butterflies." This is normal. And those who succeed are those who try the thing *in spite of* the butterflies—who concentrate more on what it is they are trying to do than how afraid they are. If the novice is so afraid that he can only think of his fear, he may easily lose himself in the air. This is not serious, but it means that he is not psychologically ready for this particular step. He would be wise to go back and rebuild foundations.

There are some older beginners, college age and upwards, who have great orientation trouble in the somersault area. In many instances they have not had previous experience in being upside down to any degree, much less turning all the way over. And the sense of physical caution does grow greater with the years. It isn't at all that an old dog cannot learn new tricks, but that he is afraid to. If this is the case, then the somersaults should be worked into slowly and with care. The youngsters will take to the spins with great gusto and much more ease.

E) FORWARD SOMERSAULT WITH APPROACH

Initial Instructions:

You have a comfortable standing somersault, with fair height, fair form, and the break somewhere near vertical. Now add your regular approach and takeoff, again not changing your hip lift force or speed, but easing out of the somersault a little more cautiously since you should have greater height.

Details and Coaching Points:

The lift of the forward somersault in tuck position is basically the same pick-up of the hips as felt in the front jackknife. The combination of this pick-up and the hard throw into the tuck gives height and speed to the spin. The teacher must remind the diver of the hip lift and slight cut back feel into the spin, or else the diver will tend to roll the somersault. "Upward arm lift and then tuck" is another fine point in mechanics which enhances height and spin. It is the same in reverse as for the back spin.

Forward somersault from end of board (series)

The break should be clean, not gradual, into a line just short of vertical. The more height the diver obtains, the "shorter" must be his break, since he will have a greater drop after the turn is completed. The diver learns to make this break into good body alignment. Hands never lose contact with the legs, but from their position on the shins in the tuck slide along the sides of the knees to the sides of the thighs. Abdominals hold firm as the body reaches extension so that the body will not carry into an arch. Knees must be completely extended, toes pointed throughout.

Common Faults and General Corrections:

These have been fairly well indicated throughout this dive discussion. Naturally many errors will go right back to the hurdle and takeoff. When in doubt as to the source of trouble, go back to the basic takeoff balance and timing. When spring coordination into the hip lift is faulty, practice on forward jackknife dives, particularly standing ones.

12

Basic Dives B

1. HALF TWIST

The half twist is perhaps the most controversial in technique of all dives. There is a basic split in the methods of teaching and doing a half twist. One school of thought favors a focus to the entry point and an emphasis in action on the arm pointing to that entry point. The other teaches a much higher focus, away from the water to the sky, and emphasis on the arm pressing back at the shoulder.

Beautiful half twists can be done by both methods. Perhaps the advanced diver needs eventually to try the different methods to see which suits him best. The half twist as taught here will be by the first method: focus on entry point and emphasis on the arm pointing to the water.

Note: a series of progressive steps is the best procedure for learning the half twist.

Must Know Already:

Plain front dive to a point of reasonable boardwork and consistent takeoff. A back dive to a point of being at home in the back entry position.

A) LAND DRILL

Initial Instructions:

As student is standing ask him in which direction he feels most comfortable turning. Experiment with one arm forward, turning away from the arm. Let him decide. He may change his mind in the early stages but usually will prefer one direction or the other. The direction chosen does not necessarily relate to right- or left-handedness.

Then standing erect on the deck of the pool, practice these specific mechanics:

1) Lower one arm to forward position, center of the body (the twist will be done away from this arm).
2) Push this arm directly away from you by pushing shoulder forward.
3) Keep looking at back of hand; continue pushing shoulder, carrying twist through hips.
4) Finish half turn (let feet move). Keep watching the hand; bring arms together for back dive position; chin up.

Half twist practice on land (4 stages, described in text)

Stress the centeredness of the pushing arm; the importance of watching the hand; chin-up position on entry. Hand actually will be pointing to imaginary entry spot in the water throughout.

Details and Coaching Points:

The mechanics for a half twist on land are very hard to perform so that they are really analogous to the eventual mechanics in the air. In the dive, they are done with the body moving through an arc toward the water, which is difficult to duplicate with your feet on the ground. The other confusing factor is that a half twist does not feel like what it looks like (this is discussed on p. 126).

The student should now be conscious that a half twist is not a bend to the side, nor is it a "banking" action. Rather it is a half turn of the body, an about-face action, with no lateral bend at all. Even this early, on land, start working on not allowing any side deviation at all.

B) FALL-IN HALF TWIST

Initial Instructions:

1) Stand on the board as for a fall-in, bending forward from the hips.
2) Point one hand to entry spot, without actively pushing the shoulder. Other arm to the side and slightly back.
3) Begin to lose balance; push shoulder forward, being careful to keep the forward hand steady on the entry spot, and to keep looking and lining up the hand with the entry spot.

Fall-in half twist (4 stages, described in text)

4) Keep pushing. As water comes up, bring "away" arm *to* the pushing arm for back dive entry. Consciously drop chin back.

Details and Coaching Points:

This is a dive in which the student must have the feeling of the rotation even at this elementary stage. He will have much trouble if he rushes on to the complete dive in hopes that it will just "come" to him. Keep him falling until he is successfully dropping into this twist and feels at home in it. The teacher should observe at an angle diagonally in front of or behind the board in order to see the arm, body, and head action. Sometimes there is something gained in understanding if the diver practices surface dives, dropping into the half twist position on the descent. Or, from a position in the water at the side wall, he drops well under the surface and pushes off horizontally into the half twist position.

At this point perhaps the teacher should be aware of what this half twist feels and looks like from the point of view of the diver in the air. It feels as though one looked down and pointed at a spot with one arm, then inscribed a semicircle around that spot and dived in.

Common Faults and General Corrections:

The focus is the most common problem at this stage. Lack of focus will cause movement of the forward hand and arm, which should not deviate from the initial aim at the entry point. This lack may also cause the head to duck. For example, if the student lets his focus and head movement follow the shoulder moving back, he will get a slap on the shoulders

Head turning with twist

and back of the neck. A similar result occurs if he aims his arm correctly but at the last minute ducks his head at the point of entry (or even just underwater).

If the steady, aiming hand is allowed to slide forward, this happens:

Hand sliding forward

and if it slides under (back toward the board), this occurs:

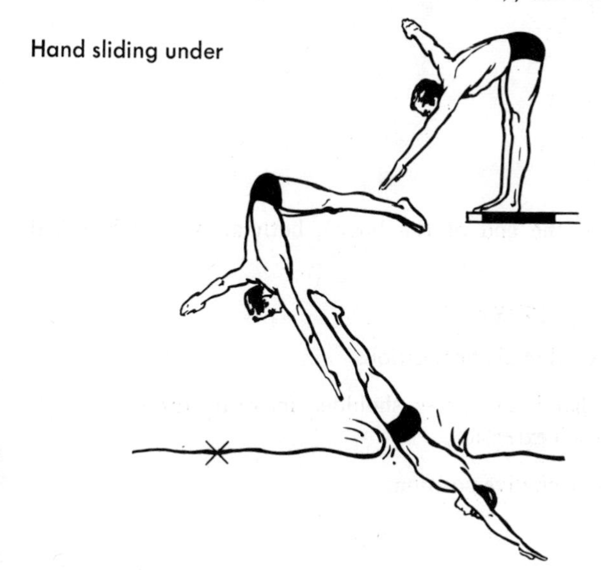
Hand sliding under

Occasionally the student forgets to bring the arms together at the finish:

Arms wide

If the diver sets his position too soon and too tensely at the start, he fails to turn at all. He must save his real shoulder push until he is falling, *allow* himself to turn, follow through with a head drop backwards and arms stretched together.

c) STANDING HALF TWIST

Initial Instructions:

1) Stand erect on the end of the board, both arms stretched and overhead.

2) Point one hand to entry spot.

3) Spring from board in above position.

4) Keep aiming hand and press shoulder forward; drop into half twist as legs reach extension.

5) Enter water in back dive position.

Standing half twist (5 stages described in text)

Details and Coaching Points:

In this step the student has to judge how hard to push from the feet and hips, and how soon to put in the twist mechanics. Too much leg push or too early shoulder action will send him over; too much force from the hips alone will make him pike; not enough will make him fall flat. The real problem of the half twist begins to emerge: coping with two rotations. Should one ride over the top, then twist? Should one do both simultaneously? The feeling should be the *start* of a forward rotation, enough so that the momentum begun should be sufficient for the forward dive part of the half twist. Then concentrate on the twist, utilizing the forward rotation to slide more easily into the twist. The rest becomes a guiding and controlling action.

These points are long ahead of the novice who is working on the standing half twist for the first time. But the teacher should be aware of the problems in rotation at this stage for better correction in general. When the novice adds spring, even the relatively weak standing push, to his mechanics originally learned in the fall-in, he is beginning to face the new problem of double rotation.

D) HALF TWIST WITH APPROACH

Initial Instructions:

1) Approach the board as for any forward dive.
2) Try, on leaving the board, to think front dive, then apply twist action as now learned.

Details and Coaching Points:

When the regular approach is added, the beginner is apt to be so concerned with twist mechanics that he forgets the forward rotation part, turns over nicely in his twist, and lands flat on his back. While it is true that the twist must be initiated during the latter part of the takeoff so that rotation reaction can begin, the student had better think of it as a front dive *followed* by a half twist. When, where, and how much are questions of practice, experimentation, and coaching. A practical working pattern is to keep alternating front dives with front dive-half twists. Gradually the student will feel his balance, and, with your help, will judge his mechanics better.

There are really no other fine points which have not been mentioned earlier in the progression. Just a general comment: half twists come very hard for some people, so it may take much combined patience to "finish" the dive. And, a half twist is unfortunately one of those dives which comes and goes. A diver can be doing it well one day, and the next, fail completely. Be prepared to drop it and pick it up again, and go back and forth a good deal before it is really set.

2. INWARD DIVE, PIKE (back jackknife)

Must Know Already:

a) The back takeoff, usually through learning the back dive.
b) Front jackknife, for experience in the mechanics of the pike.
c) Back jump, which should be worked on for smoothness and balance as the intermediate step in the direction change from a back dive to a back jackknife.

Initial Instructions:

The back takeoff will be as usual. Keep in mind the feeling of the back jump as you are pressing with your feet on the board. Just as you leave, pull up sharply into the pike, driving your hips up above your shoulders. Watch entry point below; dive in.

Details and Coaching Points:

If the back jump has been well practiced, takeoff stability will hold nicely for the first attempts. The takeoff must be stable and consistent or there is no sense in trying the inward dive. It must be strong and complete. If the beginner fades out in his push on the board and chops into the pike too quickly, he may accidentally hit the board.

There is no secret to a good inward dive except this stability of takeoff, and a good hip lift into the pike position. It takes a little courage, and the student must have lots of faith in his teacher. I, personally, am strongly opposed to such nonsense as starting on one corner of the board, or allowing the beginner to twist to one side. By these devices you merely teach bad habits of flinching and wincing, plus creating a feeling that the

Inward dive

dive is dangerous, which is not true. If the takeoff is not yet safe, not a good square takeoff with proper distance and control, *then the dive should not be attempted.* It is inviting accident, and is definitely the teacher's fault if he allows it. It is a big responsibility to keep the enthusiastic beginners (especially boys) from trying these things on their own, developing permanent faults and perhaps receiving injuries.

From the peak of the dive the mechanics are the same as for a front jackknife. In one way it is easier than the front jack, since a set takeoff means fewer possibilities for imbalances. The part which is different is the part from the takeoff into the lift of the dive. The takeoff press must feel vertical, and must be followed by a feeling of picking the hips up over one's head, a shade behind the shoulders.

This inward lift is a knack of balance and timing which comes very easily to some individuals, with great difficulty to others. In a sense it is an abnormal rotation, starting the body's center of gravity travelling in its usual arc, then forcing it to go contrary to the usual direction of the backward group. It's the same idea as a reverse spin put on a rolling ball.

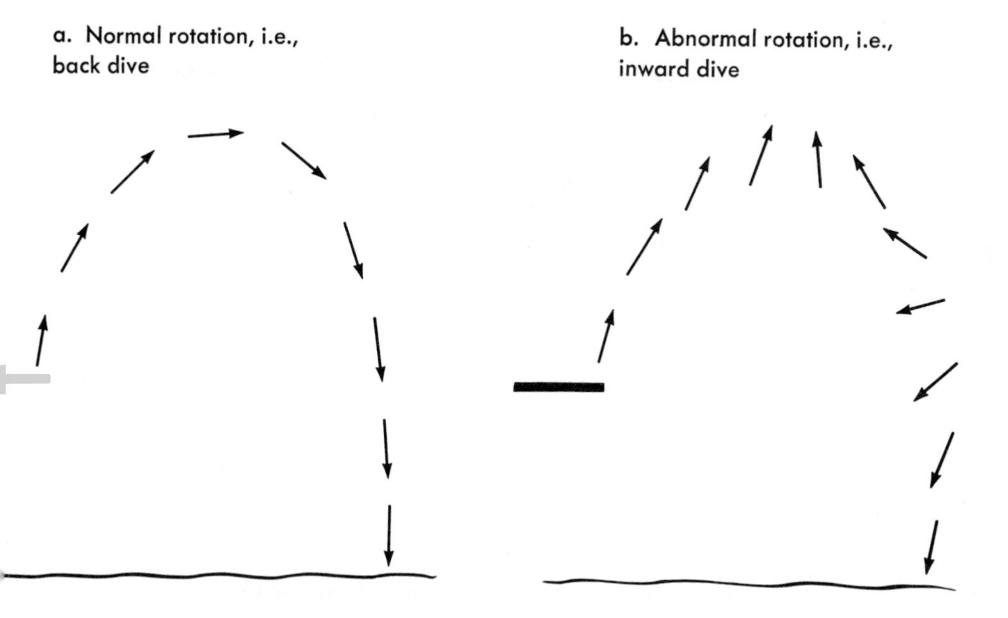

Common Faults:

The timing of the takeoff and the placement of the hips are the two large problems. The dive is easily over-anticipated and rushed, which means the takeoff extension is frequently not really started before the body is off the board. As has been explained for the back dive (p. 90), this can cause the dive to come close, and in the case of the inward dive, it is the head which is closest to the board as it is passed. If the takeoff angle is too straight but the extension has been completed, the diver will be close but will be in a position to see and catch the board on his hands. If he has hurried off without a strong takeoff extension, then he will be in trouble.

Vertical takeoff

1.

2.

3.

4.

Incomplete takeoff

Happily, most beginners have a healthy respect for the board, especially in this dive, and the usual result of the incomplete takeoff is a low pike with much distance:

Low dive with distance

Within the mechanics in the air, the faults are somewhat the same as in the front jackknife. There is a greater tendency to pull the legs forward, due to inadequate or late hip lift, a lean back on the takeoff, a lazy leg push on the takeoff, or great tension in the hip flexors. This gives the diver a "stuck" feeling, and indeed he is stuck.

General Corrections:

From the beginning of work on this dive you must be aware of the diver's takeoff balance, from the initial arm action to the final press. Watch the top of his head against the wall (or trees), and note the degree of movement and when this movement comes. This will often give you the specific cause of his distance from the board. Perhaps his inability to complete the takeoff extension is because he has leaned back so far that he's off before he can push. Occasionally a diver leans *forward* as he lowers his arms. This may make him come close, or, by way of compensation, may make him lean back too much on the press which follows.

A point to check on in takeoff mechanics is the feet at the moment of takeoff. If you see this sequence:

a. Back takeoff with late ankle extension

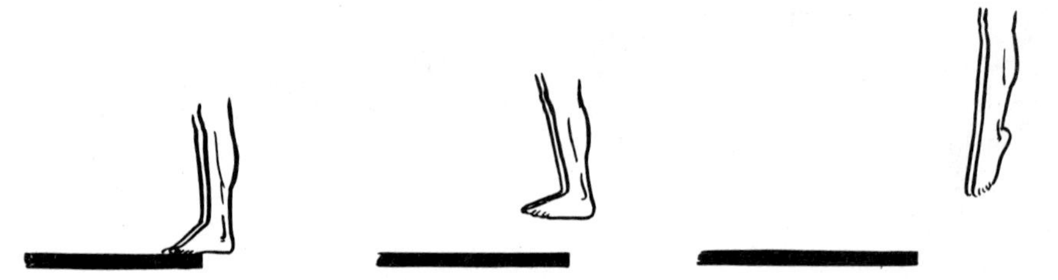

you will know that the student has not completed his push all the way through the entire foot. For complete extension power, his feet should look like this:

b. Correct foot action leaving board

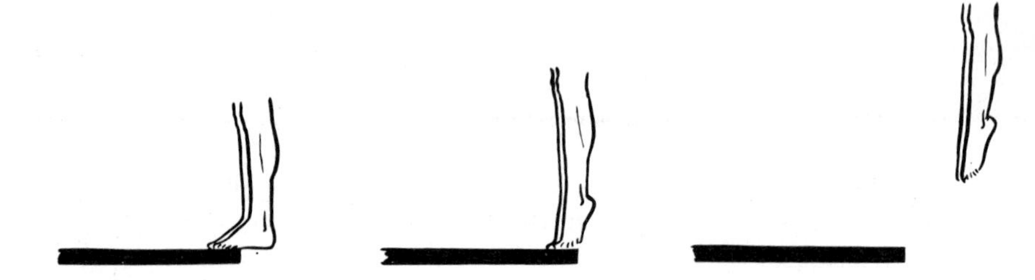

Explain this to the student and correct him on land by practicing back takeoff jumps, moving back about six inches each time.

3. SWAN DIVE

Technically a "swan" is a front dive in layout position. It was called a front header in the old books, and is called a "swallow" in many European countries. As far as we know, it is known as a "swan dive" only in the United States.

Must Know Already:

Plain front dive to a point of reasonable boardwork and consistent take-off:

Initial Instructions:

Take your usual approach. As you leave the board, lift a little at both ends; that is, pick your feet up faster and harder than for a normal front dive, and at the same time lift your head and shoulders a little, opening the arms to the side. Look for the water; close arms; dive in.

Details and Coaching Points:

Simple as it looks and sounds, the swan dive is a very difficult dive, one of the hardest form-control dives there is. Yet it is often taught early in a progression of dives. This is somewhat a matter of motivation: just as people want to learn the crawl right away in swimming, though it's no beginner's stroke, so the swan dive has the attraction and glamor in diving. It seems as though it should be easy to do. Certainly there isn't *much* to do. There is no turning over as in somersaults nor any complication of twists. That's the trouble—it is a small amount of rotation with very little in the mechanics of execution to control the dive and to compensate for mistakes.

The very simple instructions are for the purpose of underplaying the arch of the body. So many people have the notion that an extreme arch is the characteristic of a swan dive. It is more a stretch: a lift of the shoulders followed by a pivoting of the whole body around the shoulders, rather than a feeling of bending back in the spine.

The diver must reach up from the board in strong extension, with a feeling of pressing the heels back immediately after takeoff. The extended body must have this rotational impetus from the heels or a pike will result. Actually the body must rotate around its own central axis in exact ratio with the arc this center takes in its flight from the board to the water. This is controlled by the press-back of the heels at takeoff combined with the checking action of the head and shoulder lift at the other end of the body. How hard to press, how forcefully to hold the head and shoulders, how soon to pull in for the water—all these have to be felt and judged for each dive. Certain key points are: a sensitivity at takeoff for how hard to lift the head and shoulders in relation to the leg lift; a pattern

Rotation in relation to arc of swan dive

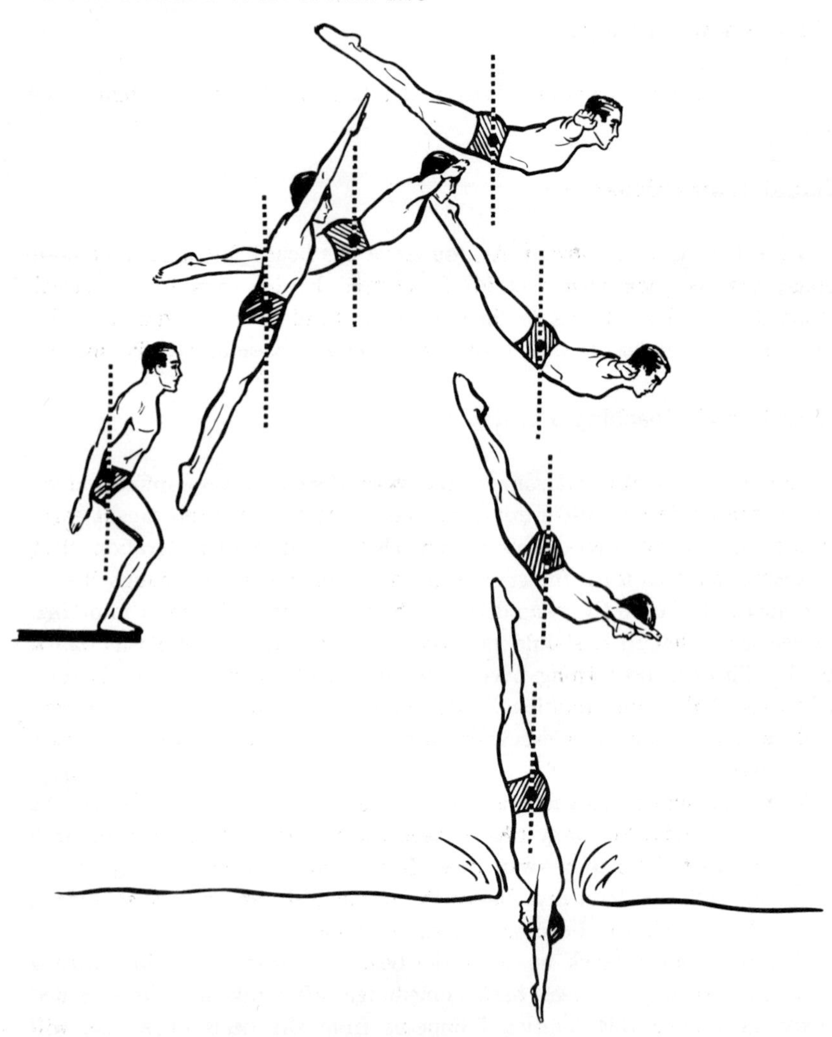

in the arm movement of an upward reach followed by the side-horizontal position; a holding of the side-horizontal arm stretch for as long as possible; a focus for entry during the last half of the dive; a stretching to the overhead arm position taking out all back arch at the same time.

Common Faults and General Corrections:

Particularly in the swan dive there are position faults which stand out far more than in any other form dive. Some of these are caused by being off balance one way or another, and some are caused by misunderstandings by the diver himself. Here is the preferred type of position:

Preferred swan dive (head up slightly,
thoracic arch, arms exactly side-horizontal)

and here are some of the common distortions:

a. lumbar arch

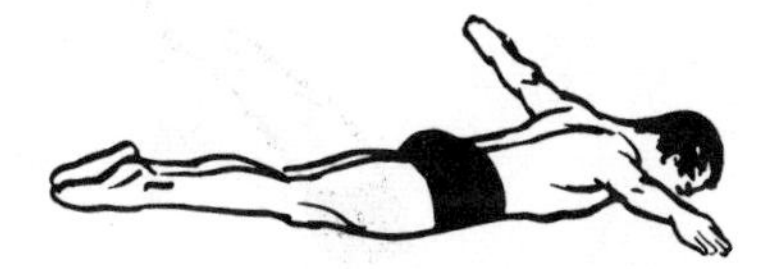

b. back too straight, head down

c. arms back

d. arms forward

In the total dive mechanics, the hard part for the diver is to set for himself the exact degree of rotational force needed, no more and no less. This is set at the point of takeoff. If he is off either way, there is little he can do to compensate or correct his position on the way down.

a. too much, arched over

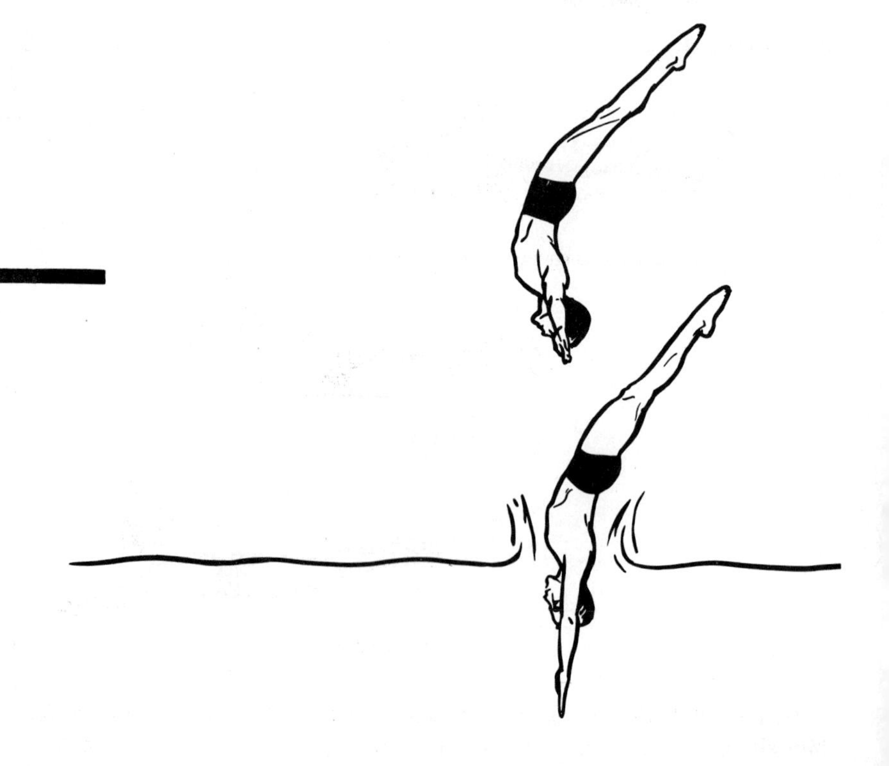

b. too little, flat entry

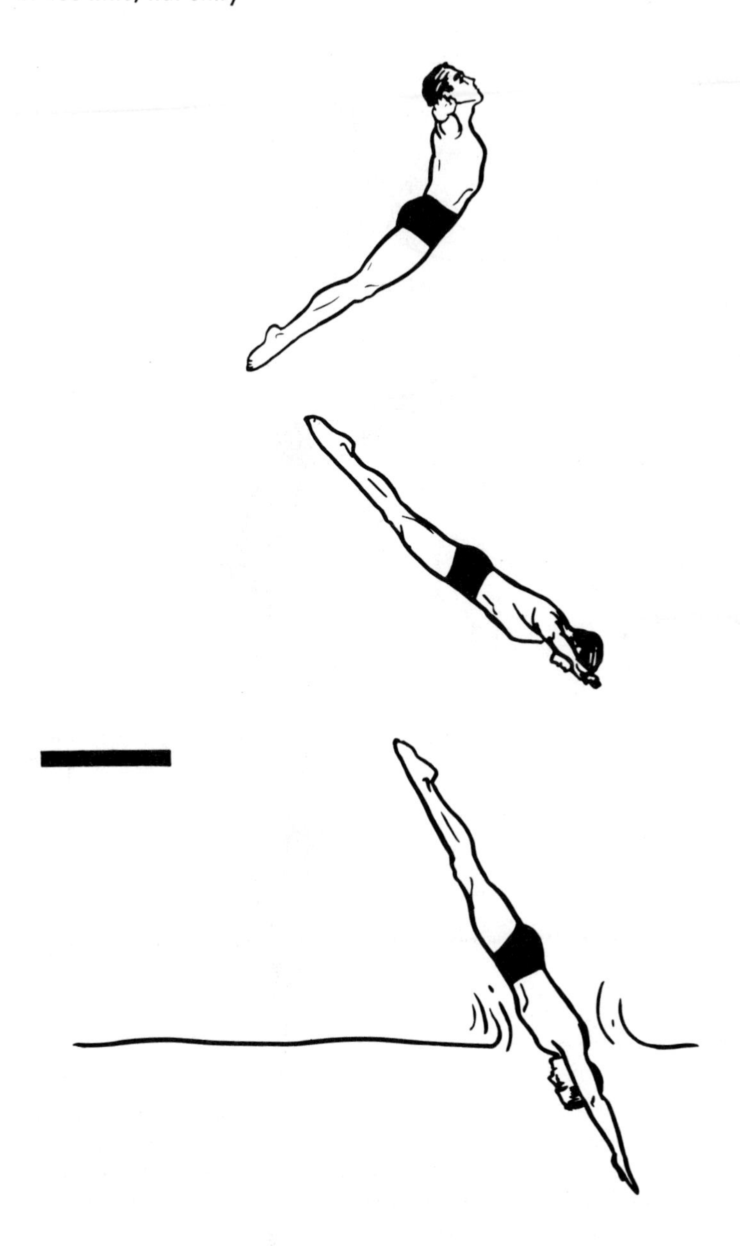

c. too little, pike for entry save

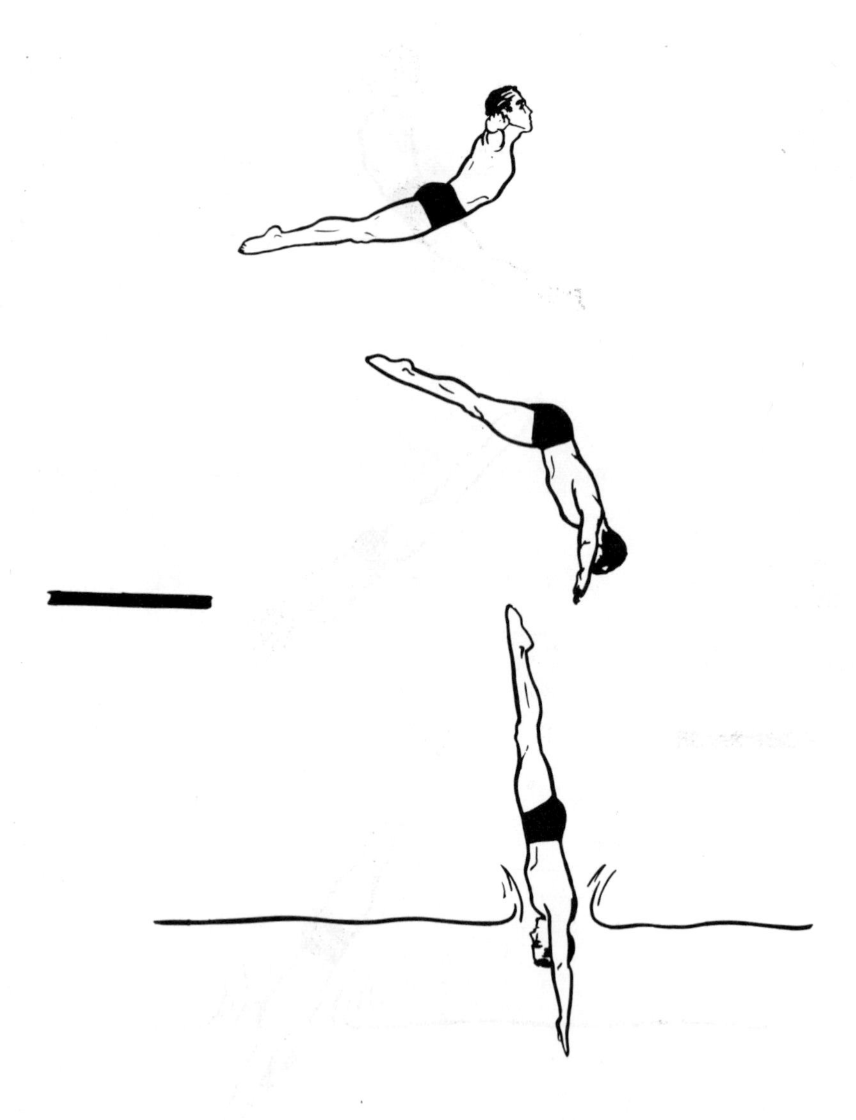

An old fashioned but effective practice is to have students lie prone on the floor, arms to side, chin on floor, legs extended. Then have them lift a little at both ends and hold the position. Correct them for back position, arm position, and head position. Rest, and repeat several times. If certain

a. lying flat on floor

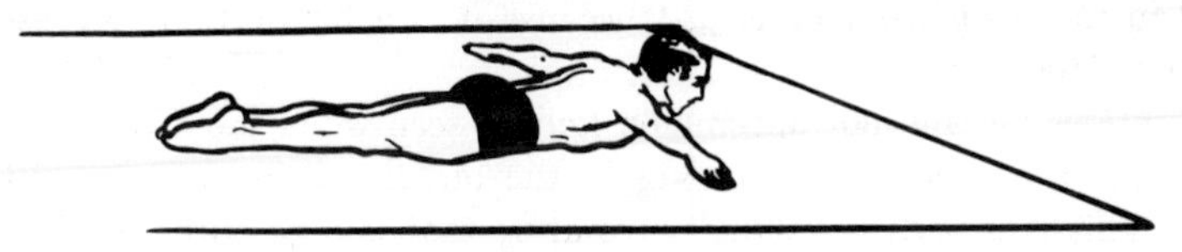

b. swan dive position

individuals have specific faults in not lifting the legs enough, or not lifting the head and shoulders enough, these things can be isolated and corrected on the floor. There is great value in feeling just where the muscles should work to produce the desired result.

If in the takeoff the diver presses back with the legs too soon and fast, he will cut off many inches of height, and will cut back close to the board. This will be especially true (the cut back) if the arms and shoulders are dropped downward too fast as the feet come up behind. This is primarily a takeoff fault previously discussed in detail (see p. 71). It is reiterated

"Cut back" in the swan dive

here because it often occurs in the swan dive when it has not shown up at all in the plain front dive, just because it is a temptation to press the heels back too soon.

An interesting and not uncommon fault is seen when the diver rises into a nice position, then seems to sag in the middle as he falls toward the water. This is usually a "short" dive also; that is, one with too little rotation at the heels from the start. Instead of diving in shallow, or piking out of his difficulty, the diver relaxes the abdominals and drops into an extreme arch. This takes a flexible back, is sometimes hard to correct be-

cause those with that kind of flexibility find the sag method an easy save, easier for them to do than doing it right in the first place.

A common entry fault, not necessarily related to the balance picture, is the failure to return to an aligned body position from the slight arched position which is correct in the dive. We have been trying to avoid too much arch, but the small amount of arch which *should* be there should not be carried all the way into the water. The correct procedure is to extend in the shoulders and contract the abdominals slightly as the arms are returning to the overhead position.

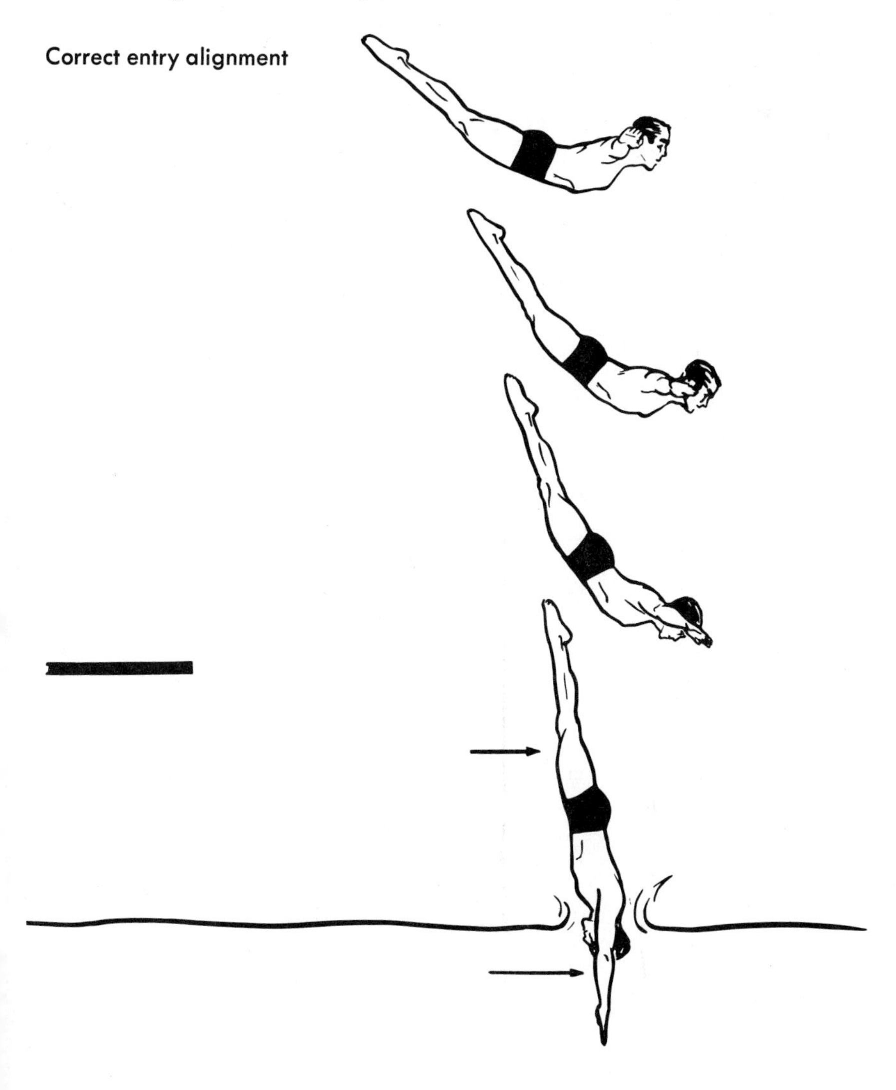

13

The Reverse (Gainer) Group

The Reverse Group, or in the more familiar but obsolete terminology, Gainer Group, merits special consideration. This group, because of its difficult direction or rotation, is one which should be approached with more than usual care for safety. With logical progression and the right mental attitude, it need be no more difficult than any other group.

As in the inward group the direction of rotation is opposite to the natural rotation from the board. Following a forward takeoff, the body turns in the reverse direction in the air; that is, back toward the board. The "must know already" requirements are:

1) A consistent, safe forward takeoff with no tendency to cut back and no forward lean of any large degree.
2) Back dive and back somersault experience.
3) Practice in front jumps to a point of reasonable height and control.

This group is usually left until the last in diving progression, and yet the teacher should try not to let apprehension grow concerning it. One certainly must wait until the diver is ready for the reverse group, but try to avoid exaggeration of its difficulty.

One can begin with the reverse dive (half gainer) in pike or layout position, or the reverse somersault (full gainer) in tuck position. The choice should be made according to the preference of the diver. The reverse somersault is technically easier than the reverse dive, but must be based on a good back somersault.

A) BEGINNING WITH REVERSE SOMERSAULT

Choosing the reverse somersault, the beginner works on jumps with a high arm reach, then jumps with a hip push forward giving him a slight rotation in the reverse direction ("long" jumps) as described on pp. 91–92. In this instance it will help to have him keep his arms overhead right through the entry. This slight reverse rotation should be accomplished with no arch in the back and no flexion at the hips. It can be

Reverse somersault

practiced from the side of the pool with advantage. The mechanics involve a strong press forward from the gluteal muscles with the abdominal muscles held firm, the press taking place from the takeoff as the body pushes upward. The head remains in line with the spine as a whole.

When this "long" jump is consistent and the diver is relatively confident, he may try the reverse somersault. It may help him to do one or two back somersaults just before his first reverse try. He should take his usual approach, have a good reach immediately followed by a hard drive with the knees into his back somersault in the reverse direction. As he turns over, he should see the water below just as he does in a back somersault, and break.

The first real try is often disappointing, primarily because the novice tends to rush into the somersault and omit the upward reach following the takeoff. An alternation of jumps and somersaults should help, if the diver can be induced to keep the lift into the jump as the start of his somersault. As he improves he can be coached for increasing this reach and lift into the spin, and on the exact timing of the break.

Be sure to let the beginner know exactly how far he is from the board. If he *is* close, he should know this and not be lulled into false security. Do not let him try the reverse somersault without your presence until you are sure that he has the confidence and skill to be safe.

B) BEGINNING WITH REVERSE DIVE

In the situation where a reverse dive (pike or layout) is preferred, the early progression is identical: practice on jumps and "long" jumps. A few teachers recommend a kicking upward of one leg in trying the first reverse dives, making the start of the rotation easier. This I have not found necessary, and I would question the practice as detrimental to the normal takeoff and to the learning of a true hip press in the takeoff.

1. REVERSE DIVE, PIKE POSITION

Sometimes an individual diver is more at home and more skillful in the pike position than in the layout position. And sometimes a coach believes in teaching the reverse dive in pike initially rather than starting with the layout position. A definite action is easier to learn than a gradual position change; for example, a front jackknife is easier than a swan dive.

It will be of great advantage to have learned the back dive in pike position first (see pp. 161–164). Then the transition to the reverse direction is relatively easy: a strong press and lift, followed quickly by a lift from the toes into the pike position; straighten back looking for the water. All the points of control are the same as for the back dive pike.

Reverse dive, pike position

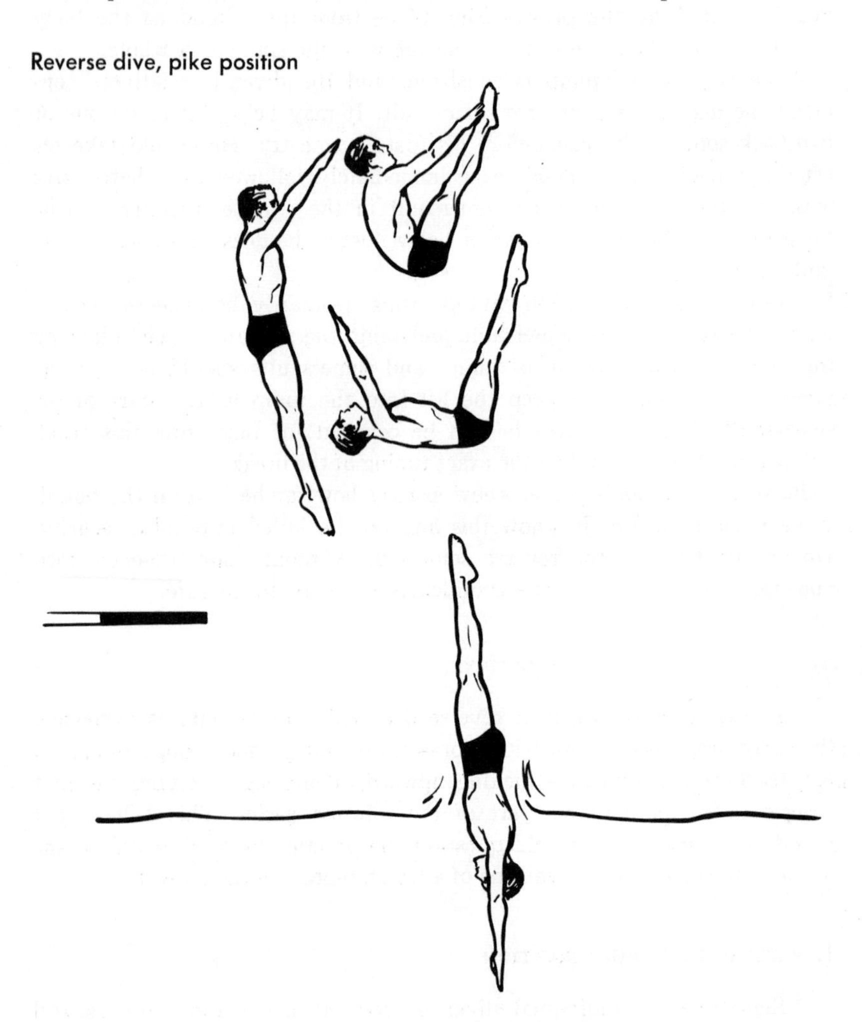

2. REVERSE DIVE, LAYOUT POSITION

In the layout position the student should go for a high jump with his hip press harder than usual for the "long" jump. He must complete the takeoff extension with a start of strong hip action before dropping his head back, or the low level of his legs will counteract his reverse rotation.

Any hard and early pull back of the upper body before complete leg extension and hip press may also cause him to come close to or hit the board. The timing from the takeoff into the hip press is very fast. Started a split second too soon, the diver will cut back; a split second late and the diver's hip press will be ineffective.

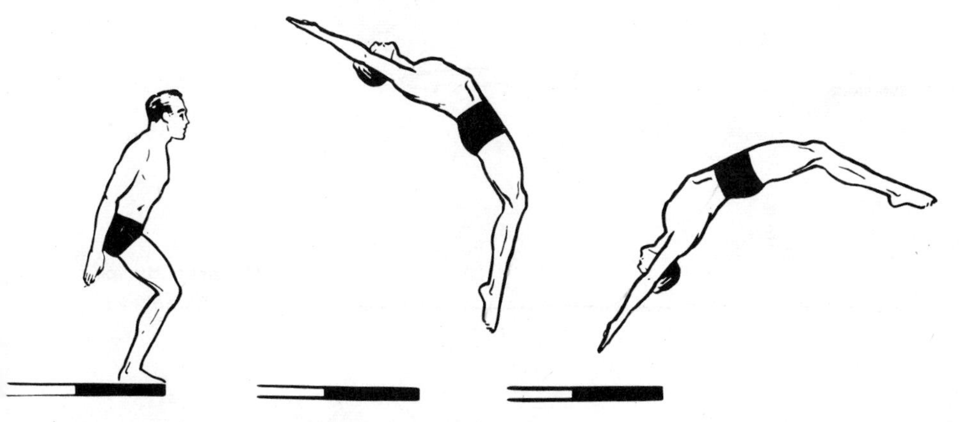

a. Hip press before leg extension is started ("cut back")

b. Pulling upper body back before hip press

c. Hip press started too late: ineffective

d. Hip press too hard and too long

Correct reverse dive layout

These problems in the timing of action from takeoff to rotation are the same for every dive in the reverse group. The success of the dive is determined at the very beginning in the exact balance of takeoff and lift from the hips. A lean forward will make it almost impossible to achieve hip press in the reverse direction. A lean backward will either cut height and bring the diver over the board, or will make him overcompensate by a sudden surge forward on takeoff extension, causing the same difficulty as the constant forward lean.

Takeoff direction faults

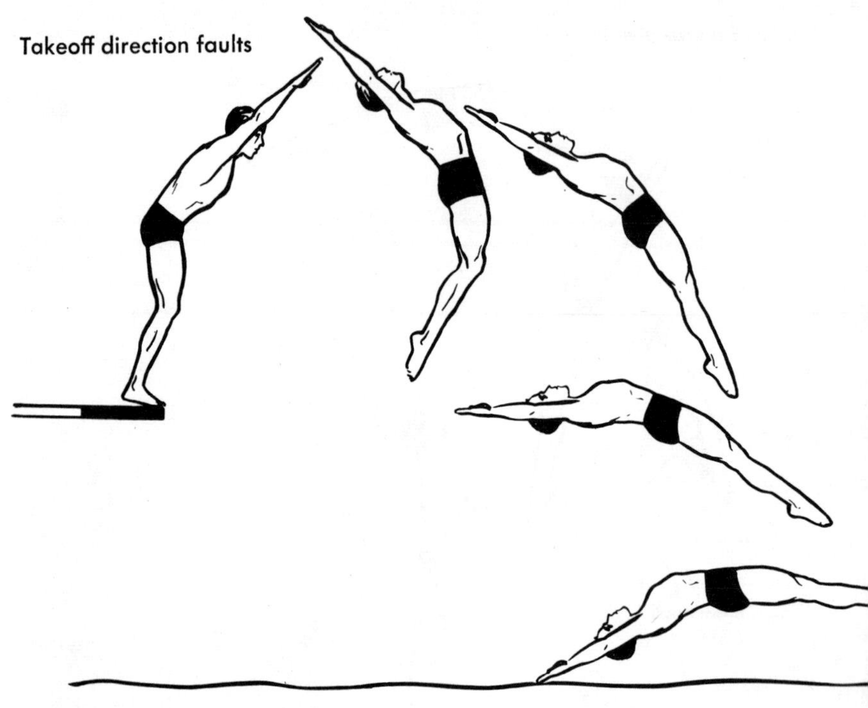

a. lean forward, dive incomplete

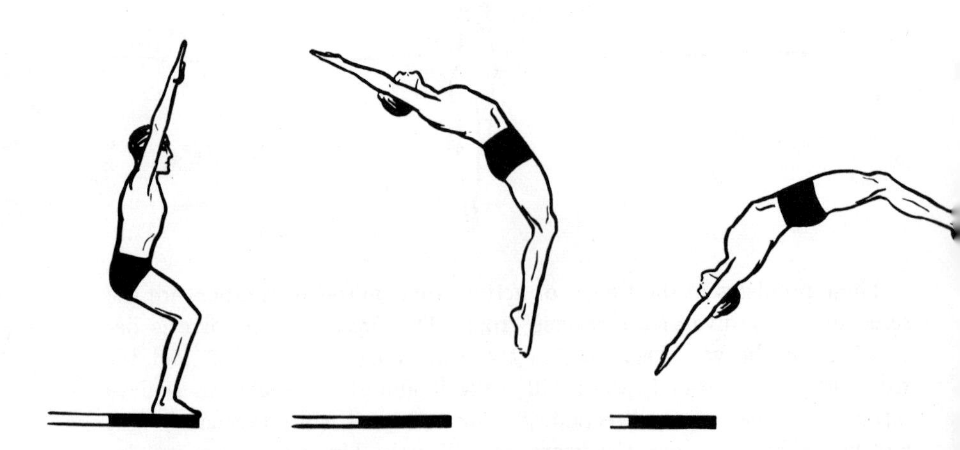

b. lean back, diver over board

c. lean back, overcompensated: dive incomplete

For maximum height and security, the diver will learn that he must set his angle of takeoff and lift very slightly out (forward), but not too much. Looking straight upward in the extension phase of the takeoff helps. Then, as the body reaches horizontal, the head drops back, the board tip can be seen, followed by the water below for entry aim. The mechanics of the dive from the peak downward are identical with those of the back dive.

At first the arm position should be overhead throughout. As the dive improves, the open position of the arms offers the same control as for the back dive (p. 93).

The reverse dive in layout position is considered by most to be the epitome of form and grace in diving. It is a dive well worth the patience of teaching and difficulty of learning. The problems do not end once the dive is mastered, for this is an exacting dive which is most difficult to adapt to differing springboards. An unfamiliar board with more or less flexibility than expected may confuse the diver. He must get acquainted with the board and perhaps try a few jumps before experimenting with his reverse group.

14

Additional Dives

These are some additional dives for each group which can be taught to intermediate and advanced divers on the one meter board. The basic five (swan or jackknife, back dive, reverse dive, inward dive pike, half twist) should be accomplished before the additional dives are attempted. The somersault should have been learned, forward and backward, and perhaps in the reverse direction. The following dives represent a continuation within each of the diving groups but do not include the most advanced dives.

A. FORWARD GROUP

1. FORWARD ONE-AND-A-HALF SOMERSAULT, TUCK POSITION

When the single somersault can be executed with good lift, tight spin, and a real drop into the entry (that is, from about the height of the board to the water), another half turn may be added. Try for a high somersault, a harder, faster spin than usual. At the point where the diver normally straightens out for the single, hang on. Look over the top of the knees for the water below. Continue around and break for a head first entry.

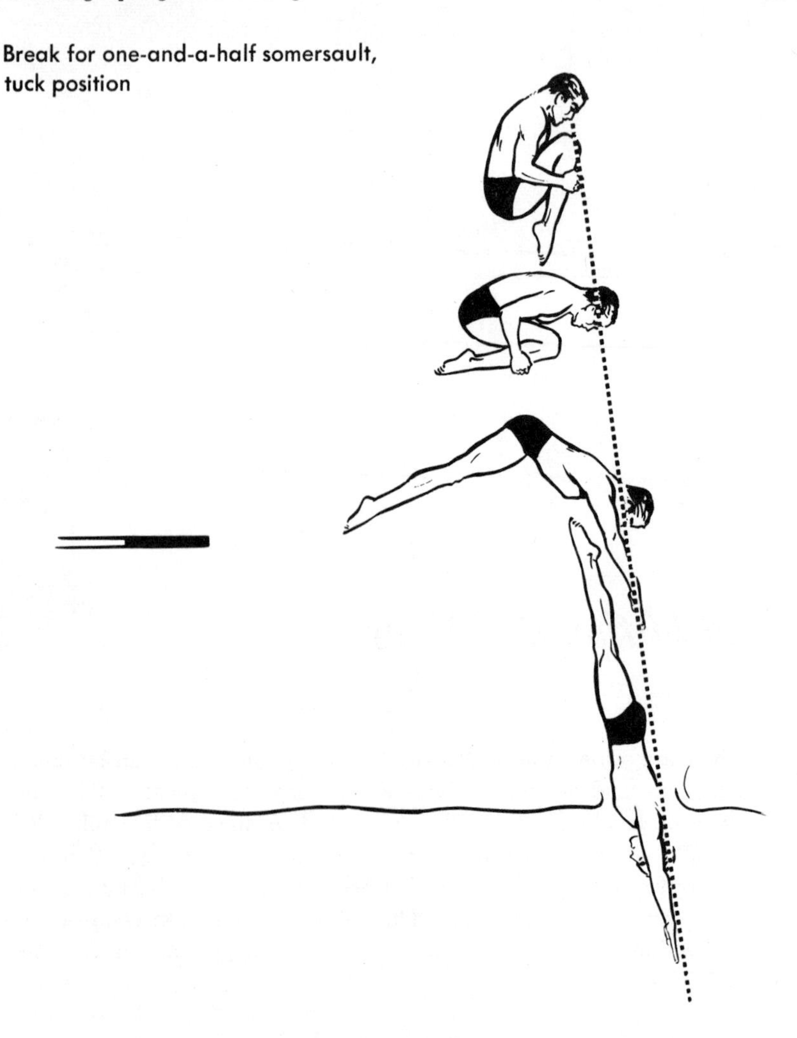

Break for one-and-a-half somersault, tuck position

After the one-and-a-half has been "made" a few times, coach the diver to try for an increased pull on the shins and a positive second hip lift as he begins to straighten out for his entry. This will give life to the break rather than allowing the body to roll into the extra half.

2. FORWARD SOMERSAULT, PIKE POSITION

This may be tried before the one-and-a-half somersault tuck if desired. The principle is a lift into a jackknife position, with three changes from the jackknife itself:

a) Head is ducked sharply and held down.
b) Hand position is behind knees, elbows bent and snug to the thighs (closed pike position).
c) Legs are pressed forcibly back instead of being held in the vertical position.

a. Jackknife at height of dive

b. Forward somersault in pike position at height of dive

The break for entry requires a stronger hip extension action than the break for a single somersault in tuck position.

3. FORWARD ONE-AND-A-HALF SOMERSAULT, PIKE POSITION

Building on the forward somersault in pike position, the same technique is used as for a one-and-a-half somersault in tuck position, now maintaining the pike position until the break. The pike position, being less compact than the tuck position, is logically slower in its spin. Therefore an optimum of height is needed for this dive.

4. FLYING SOMERSAULT FORWARD, TUCK POSITION

The principle of a "flying" somersault is a layout position held approximately to the vertical followed by a quick tuck and break. The feeling is that of a swan dive done purposely long (going over); fold into a tuck and straighten almost immediately. The centrifugal force involved in the position change from layout to tuck turns the body very quickly. The diver must have a forceful press from hips and heels simultaneously as he leaves the board, and a strong hold in the head and shoulders around which to pivot. He must fight lifting hard from the hips without equal speed and force from the heels, or he will find himself in a pike position. Once turning, he must hold the swan position a little longer than he finds comfortable (keep chin lifted firmly), then tuck.

Flying front somersault

The fly feel takes much practice. Faults lie in the pike tendency on one hand, and too fast a cut back into the layout position on the other. The latter cuts off height, rushes the dive, and may bring the diver too close to the board.

B. BACKWARD GROUP

1. BACK DIVE, PIKE POSITION

A control dive of some difficulty, this should preferably be learned before a back somersault in pike position. If the pike somersault has been learned first, the diver may have trouble making himself stop at the halfway point.

The mechanics of the back dive pike are to leave the board almost in a back jump position, lifting from the ankles into the pike position up-

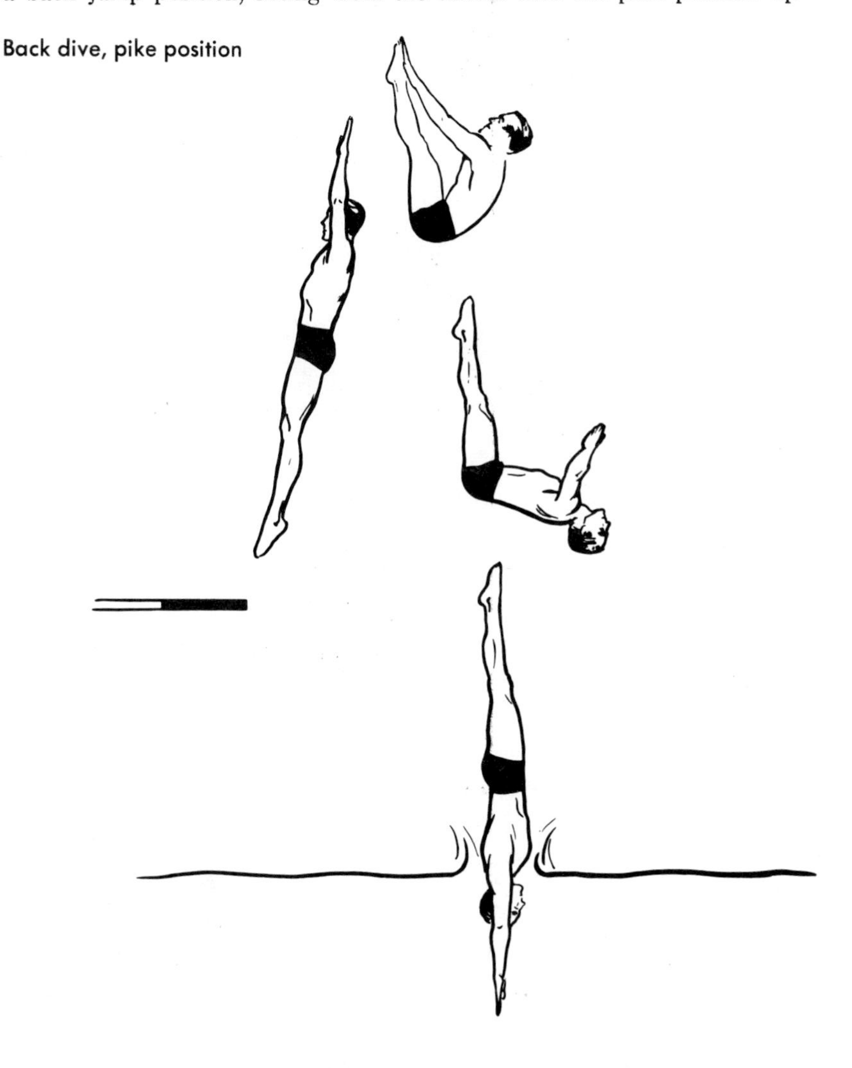

Back dive, pike position

sidedown (this to be reached by the peak of the dive). Then leave the feet where they are, straighten back with the upper part of the body for the back entry, head reaching its extended position last.

An exactness of balance in the pike position is absolutely necessary. If the legs are not high enough at contact, they will fall again at the break. If the legs are too high, they will overbalance on the break and the diver will go over.

Balance faults in back dive, pike position

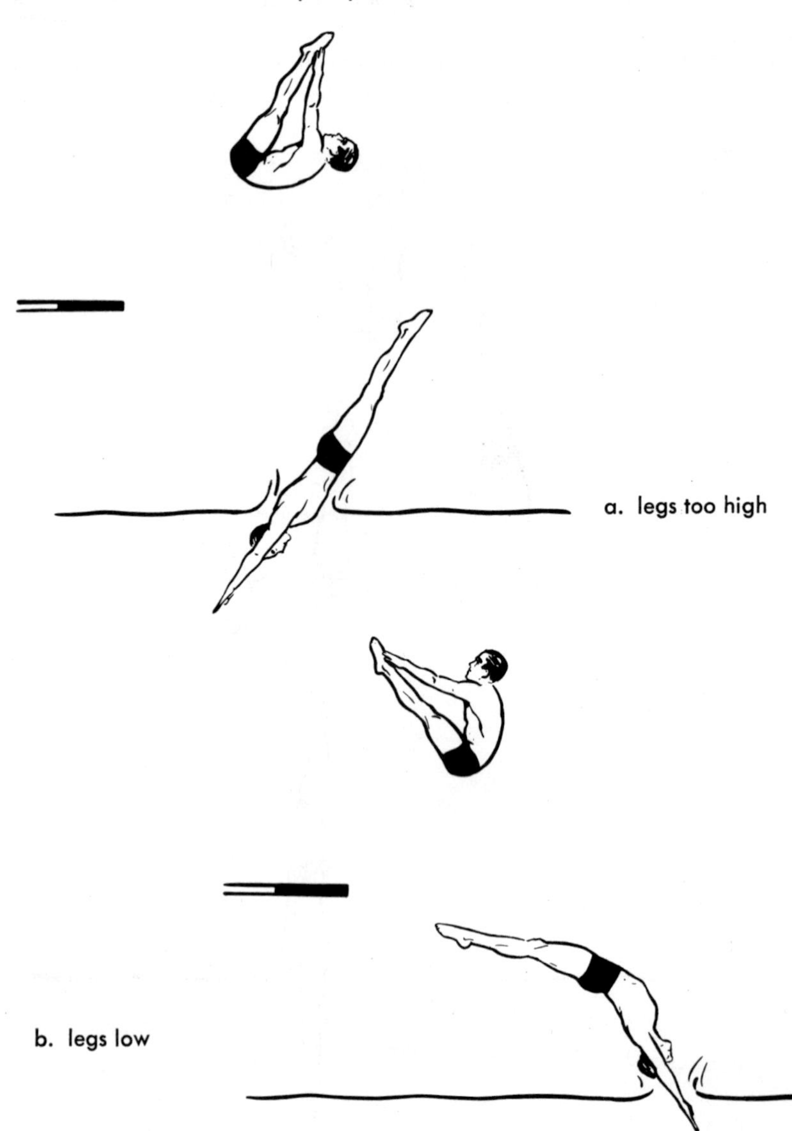

The upper body must check its normal tendency to tip backward on the rise, yet there must be no forward leaning from the upper body into the pike position. Arms reach straight up, ankles are lifted to the hands. Many divers find a point on the ceiling or in line with a tree top at which they aim their toes for best balance. Many find that in the second half of the dive, the descent, a wide arm break gives them the best control of position:

Wide arm break in back dive, pike position

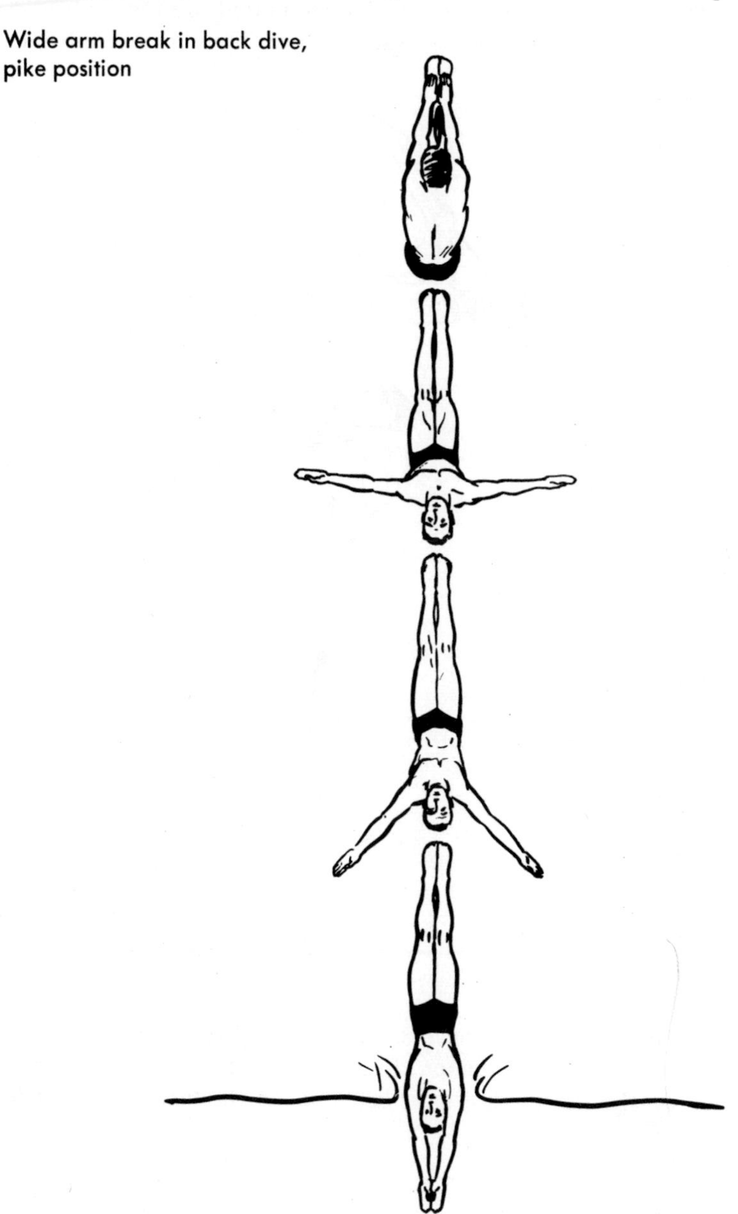

The back dive pike is a blind dive: one cannot see the water until just before entry, since the head eases back last.

2. BACK SOMERSAULT, PIKE POSITION

This is not so different from a back somersault tuck. Following takeoff, both legs are lifted simultaneously; arms reach upward, then grasp behind the knees. The body is pulled over, water sighted below for entry break.

Back somersault, pike position

Strong abdominal contraction accomplishes the initial leg lift into the pike. The head is in a normal position on the rise, chin lifts as the turn begins in order to see the water. Care must be taken on the break to make it smooth and complete: to remove the hip flexion but not continue into overextension.

3. BACK SOMERSAULT, LAYOUT POSITION

This dive stems directly from the back dive layout. The differences are in a much stronger hip press, head action and shoulder action. Once over the top, the diver sights the water and judges entry as for all back somersaults.

Back somersault, layout position

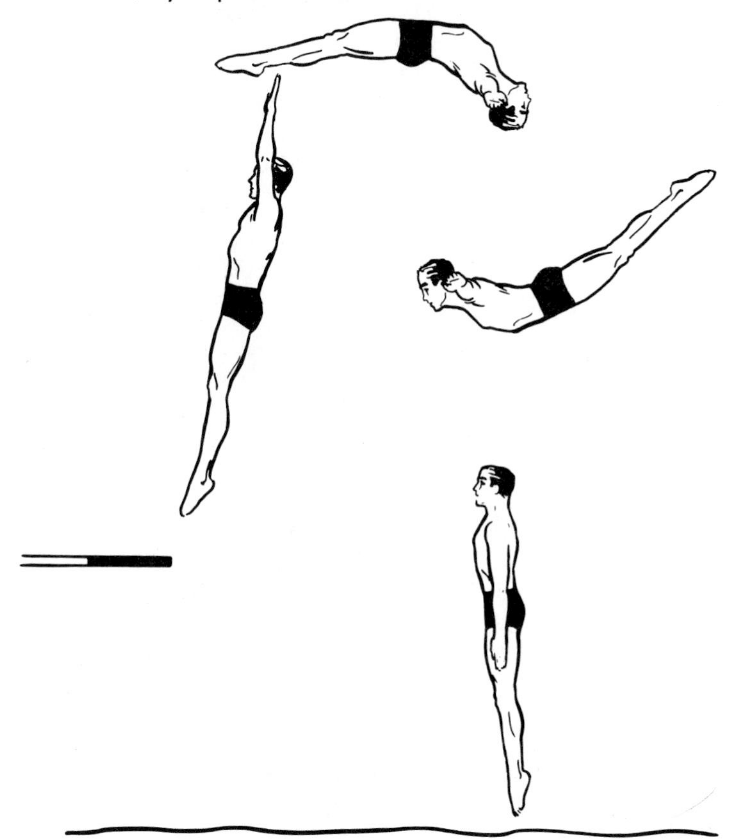

Major faults lie in lack of hip action—either in late timing or in lack of force. This will cause the knees to buckle in the attempt to get around, and a deep back arch. The takeoff into the back layout is most important.

Strong hip lift directly into the stretched out position from a good takeoff press is vital. The problem is that, should this hip lift be inadequate, there is almost nothing which can be done to compensate or "save" the dive without spoiling the layout position.

Faults in back somersault layout due to inadequate hip lift

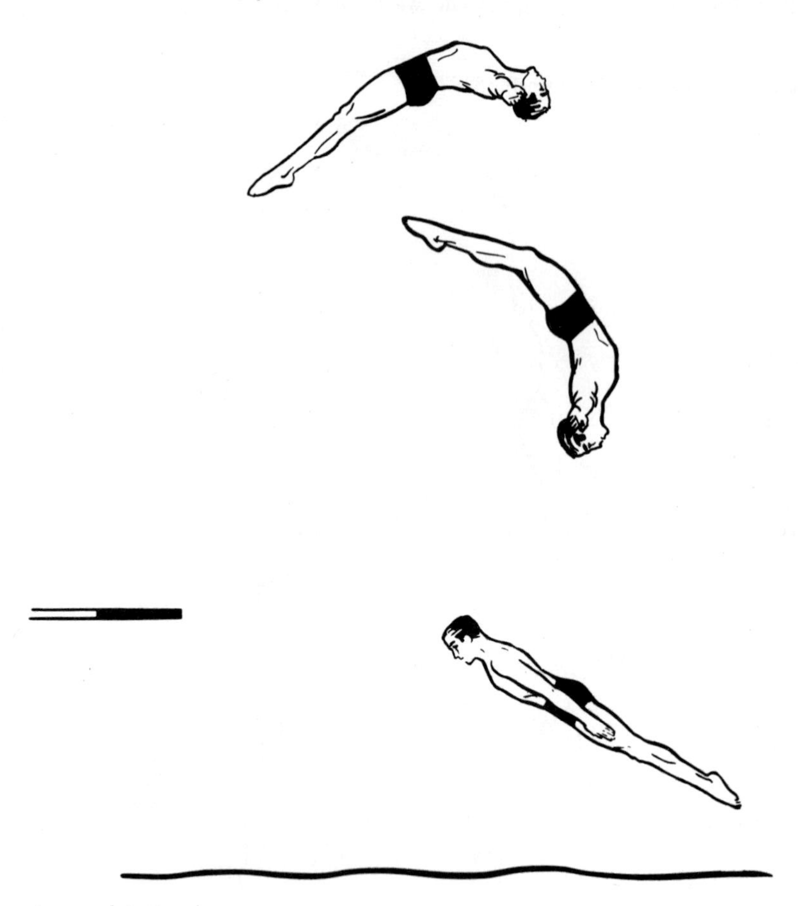

a. incomplete turn

b. pike in the break

4. BACK ONE-AND-A-HALF SOMERSAULT, TUCK POSITION

Only an advanced diver should try this one. He needs excellent height, good back spin experience, and the confidence and courage to try a new break which is blind. Practice back somersaults (tuck), letting them wash over a bit on purpose. Then perhaps try a "somer-sit" backwards:

"Somer-sit"

When the "somer-sit" becomes consistent, then try for the same, but reach back for the water at the point where the "sit" came:

Break for back one-and-a-half somersault (tuck)

If the spin is consistent, fast and high, the diver will soon learn his exact timing for the break. He must try for a high single somersault, after which the hips are lifted actively as the feet are placed diagonally upward and the diver reaches back. This second lift is a way of checking the body motion in its spin, and will make the break clean and alive.

C. REVERSE GROUP

1. REVERSE SOMERSAULT, PIKE POSITION

Many average divers are content with the basic reverse dive and reverse somersault in tuck position from the one meter board. However those who find the back somersault in pike position easy may want to try the reverse somersault in pike. They will gain a little in degree of difficulty and add a new dive to their repertoire.

The reverse somersault pike is built on two preceding dives: the reverse somersault tuck and the back somersault pike. If the reverse dive pike has been learned, this will give the diver the feeling of the straight leg lift on the reverse takeoff.

The takeoff reach and direction are the same as for all reverse takeoffs. On leaving the board the legs are lifted from the hips, arms grasp behind the knees, body turns over and entry is made. All the points of strong abdominal contraction and normal head position remain as in a back somersault pike. In the reverse direction a slightly increased distance is necessary for the body in the extended leg position in order to clear the board.

2. OTHER REVERSE DIVES

There are only a few other advanced reverse dives attempted from a one meter board, and these will not be described since they are so rarely attained in the educational situation. These are the reverse somersault in layout position, the one-and-a-half reverse somersault in tuck or pike position, and the double reverse somersault tuck. If such a level of diving should be reached, the procedure is to follow the usual takeoff technique for the reverse group and the general mechanics as described for these dives in the backward group.

Reverse somersault, pike position

D. INWARD GROUP

1. INWARD SOMERSAULT, TUCK POSITION

Based on the knowledge of the forward somersault tuck and the inward takeoff for the "back jackknife," there is nothing new to add in instruction. However, the diver must have a solid grounding in those two dives. His inward takeoff must be consistent. He must have achieved that knack of a strong hip lift which is a safe distance away, yet not at the price of sacrificing his height.

A coaching point which helps is to "think" inward dive on the lift, but *do* a somersault. Feel the same sharp pull up of the hips but allow the head to drop; the tuck is fast and hard. On completion of the single, the diver can clearly see the board—*should* see it, and judge his entry timing accordingly.

Inward somersault, tuck position

2. INWARD SOMERSAULT, PIKE POSITION

This is merely a body position change in the inward somersault, but the execution is more difficult than this one change might indicate. It takes a stronger hip lift, a little more distance from the board, and the initiating of a slower spin in a direction which is contrary to the natural takeoff tendency. Only those who find forward pike spins easy and who have shown great facility in the inward direction should attempt this dive. It is essential to learn it if the diver is working for a one-and-a-half somersault in pike position from the three meter board.

Inward somersault, pike position

3. ONE-AND-A-HALF INWARD SOMERSAULT, TUCK POSITION

If the diver is doing excellent single somersaults tuck in the inward direction with good height and considerable time to spare, he might try the one-and-a-half in this group. He must maintain the same good lift and spin, then carry around for the second pickup of the hips at the break for a one-and-a-half. This will be identical to the forward one-and-a-half somersault except that it is more difficult in the inward direction.

Inward one-and-a-half somersault, tuck position

E. TWISTING GROUP

This group has great scope for addition, since a twist added to *any* of the other dives from any group puts it into the twisting group as a different dive.

1. FRONT JACKKNIFE, HALF TWIST
(forward dive, pike position)

This dive has a vastly different feel from the half twist in layout position, and there are few divers who accomplish it as easily.

A jackknife is executed with the initial action slightly faster than normal, and the leg position just a bit forward of the normal pike for a jackknife. The twist is accomplished as the body straightens, beginning

Jackknife with half twist

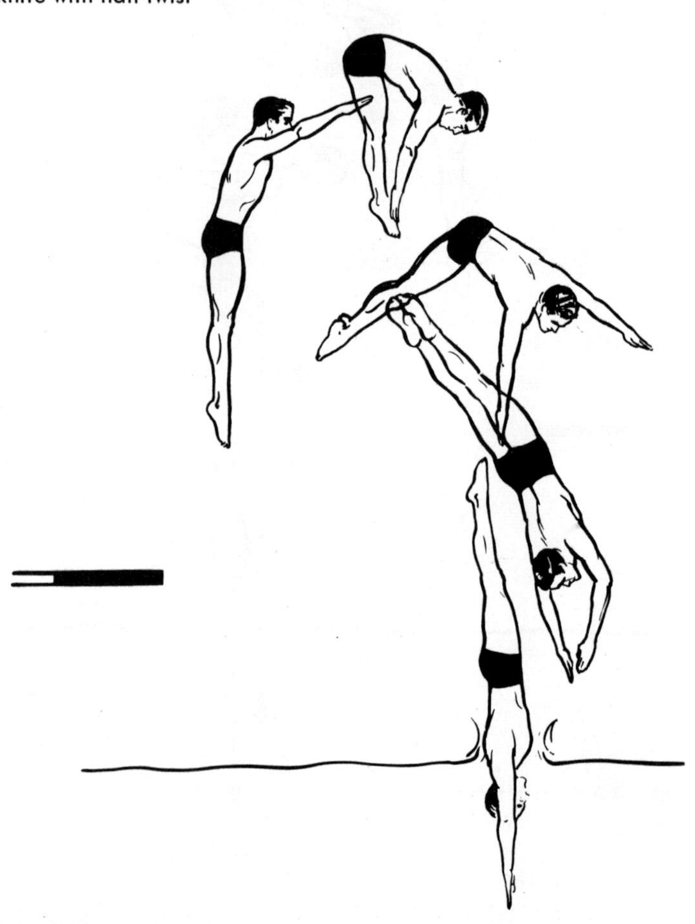

more from the hips than from the shoulders. Head and shoulders act as direction stabilizers. General mechanics are similar to the half twist layout: point hand to entry spot, drop and ease into twist simultaneously. The twisting action is slightly faster, since the pike must first be completed, and the arm spread is not so wide.

2. BACK DIVE, HALF TWIST

Although it is a very pretty dive, this one is seen infrequently today. At one time (1939–41) it was a required dive in A.A.U. competition. It is a dive which is a challenge to control and balance, and has a lovely feeling.

The diver must have a good consistent back dive layout. If not, he will find that the twist attempts may confuse his unsettled back dive and he will have much trouble with both.

Back dive with half twist

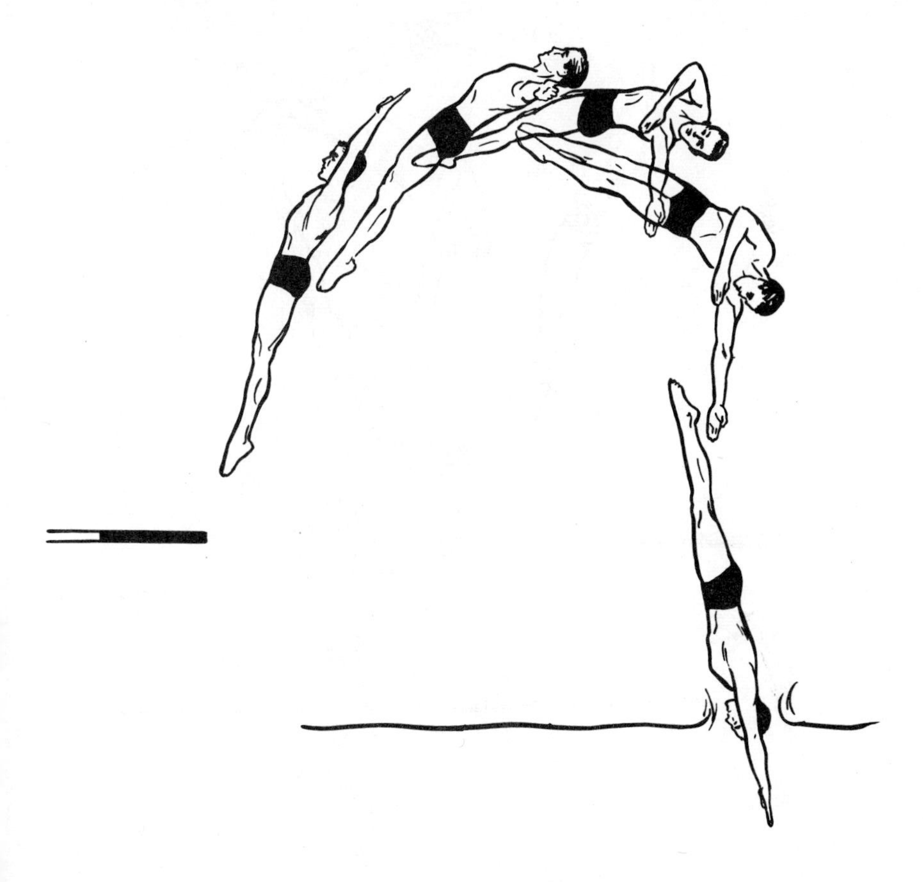

The idea is to lift from the board with only a slight backward tendency, head in a normal position looking straight ahead. At the peak of height, turn the head over one shoulder to look for the entry spot below, and at the same time cross one hand under that same shoulder to assist twist. This hand should stretch to entry point immediately and the other hand line up with it. Strong mid-body control must be held to twist easily and not get involved with piking or arching compensations which prevent twisting.

As the twist is in progress many divers take a wide spread arm position, as in a swan dive, which adds to control of the twisting action and enhances the beauty of the dive.

3. REVERSE DIVE, HALF TWIST

In essence this is identical to the back dive half twist, now taken in the reverse direction.

Reverse dive with half twist

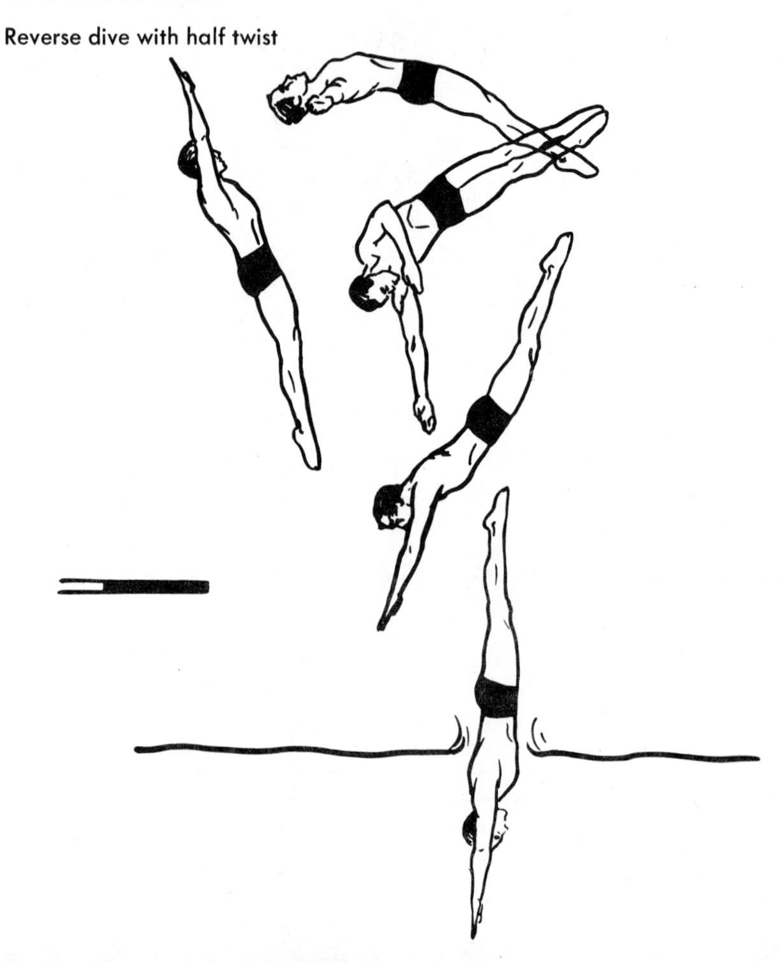

4. REVERSE DIVE, HALF TWIST, FORWARD SOMERSAULT TUCK

Taking a high, fast reverse dive half twist, fold quickly into a tuck somersault forward at the completion of the twist. This is an advanced dive, and requires a knack of fast direction and position change, and great balance sensitivity. The rise into the reverse layout, through hip press, must be high and executed with greater rotation speed than the plain reverse dive; then the half twist must be done quickly, almost snapped around. At this point the legs should be at least vertical, so that the mechanics of the tuck are as they are in a flying somersault, now done in the inward direction.

Reverse dive, half twist, forward somersault tuck

This dive may be approached through playing with the back dive half twist with forward spin added. The advantage of the stationary takeoff in the backward direction allows the diver to feel more secure in experimenting with new mechanics in the air.

5. FORWARD DIVE, FULL TWIST

A deceptively difficult dive, the full twist has been attempted and abandoned by many excellent divers.

General mechanics are a high fast front dive followed by a swing of one arm under a shoulder, continuing around to entry position. The body is carried in one full turn around its vertical axis. The twist is stopped by checking with the second arm as both line up for the entry. The head does a "spotting" action as in dance turns: keep looking at the water (entry point) as long as possible, then turn head fast back to the water over the other shoulder.

Full twist

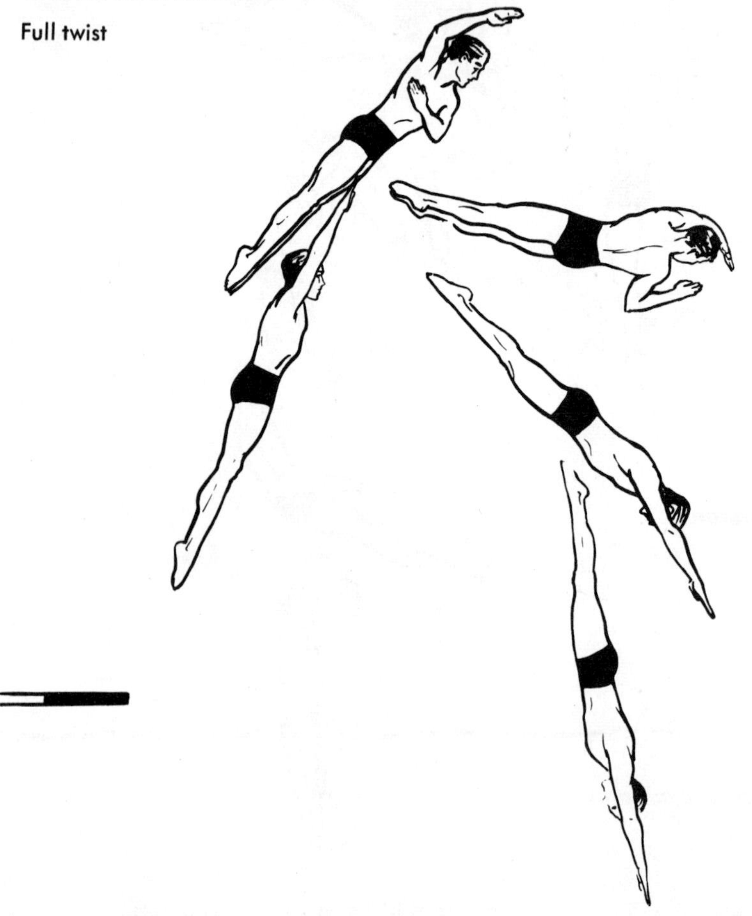

There are other variations in technique possible. A half twist action can be followed by a fast head turn to complete the twist. Occasionally, divers accomplish the twist in the hips and shoulders without taking their arms from an overhead position.

6. OTHER TWISTING DIVES

Many other twisting dives exist for those ready for them, and particularly for those working on advanced three meter diving. These dives lie mostly in the area of twists combined with somersaults, and for these the author would recommend more advanced references.[11, 12, 13]

---

[11] Moriarity, Philip, *Diving* (New York: Ronald Press, 1960).
[12] Armbruster, Allen and Harlan, *Swimming and Diving* (St. Louis: C. V. Mosby Company, Third Edition, 1958).
[13] Clotworthy, Robert, *Diving* (New York: Thomas Nelson and Sons, 1962).

15

Transition to the Three Meter Board

Where several heights of boards are available, it is advisable to begin diving work on them as soon as possible. A diver taught only on a low board with other boards in sight will begin to think there is something very dangerous about the higher boards and may develop a long lasting fear of using them. There can be hazards in experimenting too soon, however, and caution should be taken with the daredevil types who want to show off "upstairs" before their skills are safe. Rules restricting higher board work should be strictly enforced until the instructor gives the word.

In discussing diving technique from boards higher than the one meter board, we are assuming this will be a three meter board (approximately ten feet), which is the standard height for a second board if there is one. Diving techniques for odd heights such as five or seven feet will be slightly modified but similar. In fact, the best setup is where there is an in-between-height board as well as a standard three meter board, and the transition to more height can be made in easy stages.

What are the differences in diving technique from lower to higher heights? Basically very little. Dive action is supposed to be executed between the takeoff and the point at which the diver passes the board on his way down. Thus the boardwork and the action to be performed should be identical whatever the height of the board from the water. The change comes only in an earlier check for entry, greater muscular control during the longer drop between the board and the water, and a more firmly held entry position for the harder impact on the water. The esthetic value of three meter diving is in the longer held positions of the form dives so that they are seen longer, and in the greater ease of completing more rotations in spinning dives.

A misconception of most beginners is that dive action is much slower and easier from a board three times as high as their familiar low board. In reality one should start the dive from the higher board with just as much force as on the one meter, then ease off for the longer drop. If the early action is not initiated as usual, the dive will never reach the proper rotation speed at all. One should remember that the rise from the board will be the same as from the low board; that is, the height which the diver attains above the board level. The fall will be accelerated somewhat, due to the greater height of the board.

When is the beginner "ready" to try the three meter board? The guiding rule is never to try anything on the three meter board until one can accomplish it consistently on the one meter board. Along with this goes the desire and the confidence to try it. Certain dives seem easier to do from the greater height in the sense that one has room to sneak them in between the board and the water. In this way the eager show-off will "get in" jackknives, somersaults, or inward dives by cheating—with little spring and no height, but a reasonable entry. Too frequently he will accomplish these because of the extra board height when he is quite unable to complete the same dives from the one meter board. This is very detrimental to his diving development and should be severely discouraged.

Back to the beginner: as on the low board, the first thing he should try is a fall-in. This can be done very early, even when he is still a beginner, providing he can do a good low board fall-in. The technique is exactly the same on the high board, with the exception being a much longer hold as he drops through more space. There is a stronger abdominal check and body stretch; and arms and shoulders must be held much more rigidly at the point of entry to cope with the greater force of impact. All the earlier coaching points hold: deep hip flexion, eyes on entry point, body lining up with head and arms. Stress particularly the complete lack of push-off—a real *fall.* The slightest ankle push from this position at that height will take the diver far beyond the vertical. A bad overthrow will not only be frightening but can cause real back injury. It is easy to control if the fall-in is true, and if the beginner will keep his eyes open and really aim for his entry.

The beginner should work on fall-ins for a fair length of time, particularly if the high board fall-in is inserted early in the general teaching.

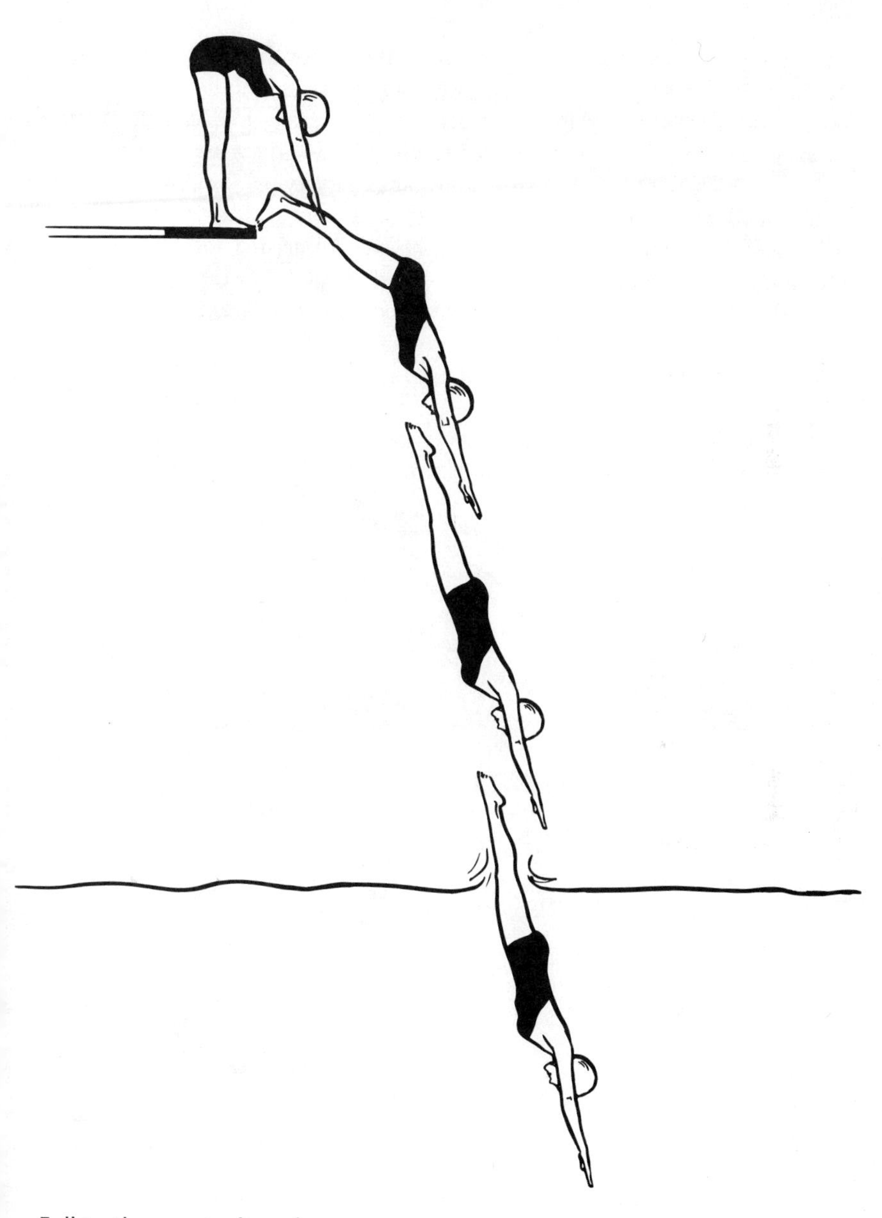

Fall-in, three meter board

Go back to work on the low board and interpolate the high board fall-in occasionally. It is wise to let the beginner try these only under the direction of an instructor for a while. If he can do them easily and can be trusted to experiment no further, he can certainly practice them on his own.

Jumping from the high board, and games involving jumping, are generally good for getting used to the additional height and impact. Jumps will not usually add much to learning the control needed for rotation, and are not recommended for any prolonged period of time because of potential harm to sinuses and ears with the foot first entry. For any who

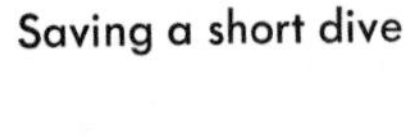
Saving a short dive

have tendencies to sinus difficulty, nose clips would be strongly indicated.

Progressing further from the fall-in, the second step should be a forward dive from an erect position with a very small push and gentle arm reach to learn to master the slower rotation. This can then be increased in degree and effort as the beginner gains confidence. Keeping the head up longer will help avoid overthrows and perhaps control exaggerated leans. The novice should know that he can always "save" a dive which has too little rotation by bending on the way down. Once he starts swinging over, he just has to take it!

From the standing dive done with fair consistency the novice can add the approach—gently and tentatively at first—then with the same force as from the low board with a much earlier check for entry and a more careful aim farther out. Go back to the analysis of the low board forward dive for faults and corrections (Chapters 7 and 8). Everything will be the same with the addition of the early check and entry control. Coaching is easier in the sense that faults are seen more clearly. Results of these faults also tend to be more drastic.

As soon as the running front dive has some ease and assurance, the front jackknife should be done. Even more than on the low board, the limited action and slow control of the plain front dive is extremely difficult to perfect. Its early placement in the progression for either board is only because it is uncomplicated in action for the beginner. The front jackknife is far easier. Again technique is identical to the low board experience, with an easing off at the break.

In starting on the back dive we meet a real challenge in teaching. While all that has been said about transfer of technique from low to high is still true, the first back dive attempt is a real test of the new diver's courage, and of the teacher's courage and ability to coach the beginner to try it, then to cross his fingers and hope. The beginner has two ill-fated tendencies: to go too far, carrying over his lowboard force into a three-quarter rotation, or, out of awareness that this is *likely* to happen, go straight up and flat down in a one quarter rotation. The problem is to accomplish the one half rotation, and the hard part is that this is done by feel, very little by focus and aim.

The first attempt should not be a back fall-in this time. As the back fall-in is done on the low board, it would carry over much too far. The head and body control necessary to stop the rotation on the way down is more than we can expect from the beginning diver. The compromise is an erect starting position, a very slight lean, a gentle push into an easy head-back position; try to see the water, and drop in.

Too much eagerness to look back will pull him around too fast. No feeling of a *hard* pull should be present, and no feeling of "arch" other than chin up, chest lifted.

When this "small" back dive feels comfortable and the diver is getting in nearly straight most of the time, the standard takeoff can be added, and more force applied. The open arm position will eventually give him better control of his body rotation. The head action going back is delayed, but should flow smoothly rather than move to the back position in one sharp movement.

With any and all of the early teaching on the three meter board, a bad

Initial back dive, three meter board

landing may have long-lasting inhibiting effects. The diver may renege on further attempts; he may compensate by rushing into dive action and neglecting his boardwork. This happens also when he is afraid of getting up any higher than the board is, or simply because he anticipates the dive action and does not allow time for lift. The best procedure is usually to go back to the same dive on the low board for further practice. In some cases the ailing dive should be repeated immediately on the high board. When the diver has been slapped but not hurt in any way, the sting sometimes so forcefully reminds him of his error that he knows where and how to correct it the next time. Other mistakes may call for a complete layoff on that particular dive and a new beginning on it considerably later. Perhaps the teacher has erred in his judgment of the student's readiness for the dive. Perhaps the student needs to rebuild confidence up to that point before trying agin. The old saying that if you miss one badly you must try it again immediately is sometimes quite wrong. If failure is repeated and repeated, that dive sometimes becomes an impossibility.

You as the teacher have to know your students' abilities and temperaments well enough to judge what should be done. This decision has to be made quickly and with assurance, or the diver will lose confidence in you.

For continued work on the high board the procedure should follow the pattern set by these basic dives described. The most important rule is to accomplish the dives on the low board first. Most dives can be carried directly from there to the high board, with an exception in somersaults. The greater distance to the water makes it very difficult to control one somersault. In the forward group the diver should progress directly to the one-and-a-half somersault tuck, provided he has tried it on the one meter first. This is an easy dive from three meters, a nice fit, whereas a single forward somersault is very hard to time. A flying front somersault on the other hand is a nice three meter dive, with the rotation delayed by the flying position. In the back group the somersault is possible in pike or layout position, but again impractical in the tuck position. A back one-and-a-half is not recommended for a start in back spins since the break for entry is blind. The single somersault tuck in the reverse and inward groups is feasible since the rotation is apt to be slower.

One final word: height causes great apprehension for some people. So ease gently into the first stages. Never force a child (or adult) to try the high board if he can't be persuaded reasonably. There are cases of real acrophobia where it is absolutely wrong to force the issue. *Compelling* someone to climb up and go off can make him refuse ever to try again. If he is ready psychologically and in his skill, he should be given his instructions, then go up and off with little hesitation. A long stalling is an indication of trouble. The barrier looms larger and larger until it is insurmountable. After a reasonable wait the beginner should come down and not be allowed to try again for a few days. In later stages of diving from the high board, balking should not be permitted. Giving in to fears and stopping at the takeoff means the diver is not ready mentally. He must be able to concentrate more on what he is to do than how afraid he is.

16

Beginning Competition

Many young teachers in aquatics are assigned the job of getting two or three divers ready for the annual water sports or camp swimming meet, or interclass school competition. The instructor often has had no direct experience with diving competition, either personally or in coaching. The following chapter is planned for those who are inexperienced in this area.

The largest difficulty is pressure: pressure in the sense of time, with a deadline; pressure from parents and friends who have all kinds of advice for the budding diver; and, to a degree, pressure from the diver himself, now highly motivated and eager to progress faster than is wise. These pressures are dangerous. They make the uncertain coach move too fast and undermine the guiding principle in teaching of building on sure foundations. There are more diving accidents due to pressures of competitive practice than anywhere else in the instructional field of diving.

The pressure difficulty can be met with patience and common sense, knowing that one competition is not to be the culmination of that youngster's progress. In assuming full responsibility the coach must have the wisdom and common sense to set his pace in the way which will best benefit the diver.

BEGINNINGS

In a situation in which there is a very limited amount of competitive opportunity, such as a young club, a school, or a camp, there are usually one or two annual events in diving requiring three or four dives. If you have the opportunity of planning these, you should select representative dives within the grasp of the group concerned. They should, if possible, represent different diving groups, and be bona fide dives—not handstands, tumbling stunts, clown dives, or jumps. As a sample plan, here is a program of weekly diving contests set up for a country club, culminating in the "medal" meet at the end of the season:

First week:	front dive back dive	Each week these dives are required, along with one or two optional dives selected as desired. Note overlapping of dives to provide continued work on them. The optional dives would include any dive not listed as "required" that week. For the culmination, the Annual Meet, the two basic dives might be returned to for the required ones.
Second week:	front dive front jackknife	
Third week:	back dive front jackknife	
Fourth week:	back somersault front jackknife	
Fifth week:	back somersault swan dive	
Sixth week:	back jackknife swan dive	
Seventh week:	front somersault back jackknife	
Eighth week:	front dive back dive	ANNUAL MEET

A larger number of dives could be included in the weekly event if suitable, and progression in adding new dives could be faster. The theory is to keep building the repertoire gradually, to keep challenging the diver safely; this in place of waiting until a few days before the big meet and trying to learn four or five new dives at once. The optional dives give the youngster a chance to use any he likes—either easy ones perhaps not required that week, or other new ones if he is learning faster than his companions.

Beginning competition should be held to the one meter board, and very definitely should not be mixed (i.e., some off one board, some off another of a different height). If the clientele on the whole has a background in diving and the divers have been working on both high and low boards, then perhaps the event could be alternated between the boards by weeks.

If a progressive program such as this is set up, stick to the rules and allow no substitutions. A diver who cannot yet execute a particular dive safely should be made to forego that week's meet if necessary. General experience shows that most youngsters will rise to the occasion providing the progression is at a reasonable rate.

"OFFICIAL" COMPETITION

By "official" competition, we mean a regulation diving event under the auspices of agencies such as the Amateur Athletic Union or the National Collegiate Athletic Association. Diving may be conducted by the same rules under other organizations such as the YM–YWCA, interscholastic or municipal groups, camps, and country clubs. Rules change from time to time, but the fundamental requirements are two dives from each diving group: five basic dives, and five optionals. This combination will cover any and all sets of rules.

Other than the specific dives, the beginning coach should also be aware of these rules:

1. In the forward approach at least three steps must be taken and a single spring from the board tip.
2. On the back takeoff a single spring must be taken. (A double spring, often called a "crow hop" [14] is a common fault to correct early.)
3. Once the forward steps have started or the back arm swing begun, there shall be no stopping, or "balking."
4. The diver must do the dive as announced. If the dive is announced incorrectly as to dive or position, the diver must correct the announcement himself before starting.

In coaching for competition the diver is developed in the same way as in instructional teaching in regard to progression and speed; that is, only as he can best take it. The observant coach will judge what positions the diver does best, how far he can succeed in the more complex optionals within his training time limit. It is far better to do simple dives well than to attempt those beyond present ability merely for the sake of the increased degree of difficulty. The score result may be the same, or may even be somewhat sacrificed, but the diving will be better and the eventual skill will improve soundly. The diver who competes with dives only half learned, practices and learns faults which may jeopardize his eventual mastery of them.

---

[14] See p. 87.

The coach must be very aware of his diver's temperament and his physical capacities: know when to "push," when to ease off; know when tension from cold or wind or nervousness is enough to cancel out the wisdom of a longer workout; distinguish between fear and laziness, between real fatigue and psychological uncertainty. All competitive divers have to be show-offs to a degree. Self-consciousness and self-deprecation must be eliminated in order to concentrate solely on the dive execution. Yet merely showing off without any foundation in skill will not produce the desired results.

All along there must be a constant exchange of questions from the diver and considered opinions from the coach. The diver must eventually stand alone in his diving, and the coach must take the more difficult and nerve-wracking position of spectator. He must be a thinking, judging spectator however, recording mentally the faults and the good points in order to talk them over with the diver later.

The general procedure in the few weeks before a competitive event is logical. From working many times on a particular dive, the diver should begin going through his dive series, in order, about three dives apiece. This should be a set number, and once decided, not deviated from. Hit or miss, just three front dives, three back dives, and so on. After each series, he should sit down for a rest and think through the errors. Then repeat the series as time allows. In succeeding days the series can be cut down to two apiece, and the last few days, one apiece. The "one-apiece" practice is now exactly the kind of experience the diver will face in the meet itself. It is by far the best type of workout just preceding the meet. Even if there are weak dives which need individual concentration, the time comes when it would be better to do them as well as possible once around each time. The diver must learn to keep going and not to let a missed dive throw him off psychologically for the rest of the set. In between each series he must be made to stop and evaluate the individual dives and the series as a whole. The goal is to concentrate on each dive as it comes, then erase it from one's thinking temporarily and work on the next one.

At the time of the competition the diver should warm up with a few dives—preferably basic ones which he does well, which will give him confidence. A few stretching and warming up exercises may help, especially if it is cold or he has had a long wait preceding the event. During the actual competition he should try to do every dive in turn as best he can, then dismiss it from his mind. The less he is aware of his accumulated score, the better. The less he is consciously aware of his competitor's successes and failures, the better. Worrying about another diver's closeness in score will only distract him from his own problems. Great concern about a team-mate's position may upset his own concentration. A diver seeing another miss badly or hit the board may unconsciously apply corrections to his own diving which have no relation to his own faults and spoil his own performance. He must be cold-bloodedly singleminded.

The post mortems in diving are as bad as in golf or sailing. The "what if's" bubble over. The standard reactions go from self-recrimination to accusations of unfair judging. Diving competition can be heart-breaking. It is an individual performance prey to whims of momentary psychological mood, physical well-being, and always to the vagaries of subjective judging. Knowing this, the only sane attitude is to feel one does one's best at that moment, and may the best man win. If you are not judged best, you need more work. When the score is very close it is difficult for everyone (including the judges). The real champion must win by enough points to be a clear and undisputed winner in order to gain real satisfaction.

Diving is just a sport—not life and death. Diver and coach should work hard to keep improving, but always remember that basically it is not so important to win as to dive well—to dive the very best that one can at the moment. Someone else wins? O.K., he was the better diver, that's all. Go home and work.

To lose gracefully, yet not submissively, takes swallowing of pride, admission of faults, yet a real inner determination to keep at it. To win graciously is sometimes even harder: to be encouraging to others but not conceited, to know one's skill but not rub it in. And, to know that the goal has been achieved, yet not exult too openly. Even more, to realize that this goal is won, but it is not the be-all and end-all of everything. There are many goals in life, and certainly a diving medal is a fine acquisition. Nevertheless, how pathetic to see an athlete hang on to his medals as his only achievement in life fifteen or twenty years later!

JUDGING DIVING

To be a good diving judge takes much experience, a broad knowledge of dives and the technique of diving, and the ability to make fair evaluations quickly. Notwithstanding these exacting requirements, most beginning teachers have the job of being a diving judge thrust at them in the early days of their teaching. In the small local competition he may be the only available person with any background in diving at all. One has to start somewhere, and it is best to be halfway prepared to undertake this unhappy job.

A dive is judged as a whole, from the time the diver begins his approach through his entry, including what happens under water. The rules set up for the competition should be kept in mind: the dive to be executed in the position announced; twists to be accurate in degree as specified. For rule infractions the judges must agree as to percentage of score to be deducted. Rules may be modified to make the competition less exacting for beginners, and this must be made known both to the judges and to the divers.

The number of judges is usually three, five, or seven, depending on the importance of the competition. The procedure is for each judge to score the dive on a ten point scale. The scores are added, multiplied by the degree of difficulty of the dive (see p. 102), and divided by the number of judges. In the case of five or seven judges it is common practice to cancel out the high and low judges' scores, hoping to counteract partiality or inaccurate judging. As well as one can, one scores approximately as follows:

9–10 Almost flawless
7–8 Well done
5–6 Fairly good, some major faults
4 More major faults
3 Poorly done
1–2 Very poorly done; bad faults in all phases
0 Specified dive not done at all

Scorecards may be used which are flashed by the judges shortly after each diver performs. Where these cards are not available, fingers may be held up or the scores written down by each judge. Half point scores are generally used above five and sometimes all the way, which gives the judge a little more flexibility in scoring.

Judging involves seeing a dive which takes only a few seconds, holding a picture of that dive in mind, and trying to give it a numerical evaluation. It is difficult to dictate exact values for each part of the dive—steps, hurdle, takeoff, height, execution in the air, distance from the board, entry. Each has its influence on all the other parts as they come. Poor takeoff balance resulting from poor boardwork will cut off height and perhaps cause faulty execution and entry. Takeoff and height may be excellent but the dive executed in poor form. Everything may be well done up to the break timing, then the entry is splashy. On the whole, one looks for the basic arc of the dive, for height and smoothness, with a secondary consideration for the form of the dive throughout. The entry is important but not the only criterion in scoring. Just because the feet are apart or the dive is not quite clean in its entry is no reason to discount the possible excellent height and mechanics which may have preceded.

The position of the judge is psychologically difficult. In most cases the spectators and competitors see what the judge is giving each dive. The often audible reactions will upset a beginning judge. The judge must try to do the best he can to judge each dive as he sees it on the basis of everything he knows, and let his conscience be at rest. Judges should be placed at different vantage points in order to have the dive seen from several angles. The scores can vary quite legitimately since one judge may be able to see faults impossible to be seen from other angles. For example if the feet are apart laterally, a judge at the side may fail to see it, whereas a judge slightly behind the board tip sees clearly.

A judge may be influenced by a diver's idiosyncracies in movement and he must be able to perceive basic movement pattern through distortion. He may also be influenced by his own preferences in being partial to certain positions of execution or styles of diving. Another difficulty is having to judge one's own students. This is not allowed in competitions of importance, and really should never be allowed. But so often there are no judges available except those with students in the competition, or at least there is no one else willing to take on judging. The problem is not always one of being partial to one's own divers, but of being too hard on them. A diver with whom you have worked for many many hours has faults and tendencies with which you are very familiar. You know just where to look for his failings; you anticipate them and are apt to over-deduct for them.

The only way is to take the bull by the horns, try to be honest and objective, and let the chips fall. It is a thankless job at best, but experience in judging begins to build confidence in your decisions. It is important to have good judges for the sake of the hardworking divers and coaches. And for you to *have* to judge is one way to sharpen your own perceptions and learn more about diving as a whole.

17

Accident Prevention

Journalists frequently "write up" champion divers and almost without exception highlight the accidents the divers have had. Many aquatic teachers are reluctant to tackle diving because they are afraid of causing injuries. I claim that no diving accidents are necessary—that there is no danger in diving if the teacher is alert to certain warnings and acts accordingly.

All sports entail a degree of physical risk in the strain and effort of the moment. Contact sports such as team games draw their share of body impact injuries. Dual sports such as racquet games invite overexertion and stress in returning the ball. Diving is in the category of aerial activity, leaving the ground and returning as in trampolining and some areas of tumbling.

Many factors can cause accidents, factors which involve the condition and setup of equipment, group control in the use of this equipment, the safety of the body of water, and weather factors. However this discussion will be limited to the area of body control: the points of safety in *teaching* and *performing,* with particular emphasis on the anticipation of accidents by observation of movement tendencies. Most accidents do not suddenly happen. The diver has habits which lead in the direction of danger long before the actual incident occurs.

The role of the teacher, therefore, is as a keen observer. He should not only be able to spot the body movements and balances which can lead to trouble, but also to do something about them at the right time. In theory this should be easy since in most teaching situations there is one diving board and one student performing at a time. Nevertheless in handling groups it is easy to become absorbed in instructing or correcting a few on the side while others continue to practice. The teacher must always have one eye on what is happening on the board and slow the speed of successive divers if they seem to be getting out of control.

There are three points at which a diver may have injury difficulty: A) contact with the board as he passes by; B) impact on the surface of the water when he is in a faulty entry position; and C) impact on the bottom of the pool or other diving area. Each of these three points is equal in importance and should be kept in mind in its turn for each dive performance.

A) CONTACT WITH BOARD

First the diver should be visually aware of the board tip. He should watch it throughout his steps and even in the hurdle should have peripheral sight to the tip. The beginner who looks straight ahead is not accurate in his landing at the tip and will find his balance very inconsistent.

The teacher looks for the general arc of the body's center of gravity both in the hurdle and during the flight of the dive. The arcs should be smooth, under control and continue in easy flight. Jerkiness, distortion of body position, great speed variation in steps, all obscure general alignment and spell trouble ahead. A very long pre-hurdle step makes problems in balance, either placing the diver forward or too low for the hurdle effort. Compensating to regain balance after a long step often puts the weight too far back; or, the diver may substitute hip flexion in the hurdle, disturbing alignment and balance. Either fault can cause a too-vertical rise or an actual cut back, bringing the diver close to the board (see p. 71 and p. 90). Any observed tendency to cut back should be worked on and corrected when first seen. This fault, if neglected, will definitely result in hitting the board sooner or later.

Going back to the steps of the approach, watch for a smooth, controlled walk with weight carried quickly from heel to ball of foot. Heavy pounding on the heels or lack of proper transfer of weight forward leads to poor balance and control throughout the board work. Flat-footed landings will cause the diver to skid at the end of the board if he is at all off balance. If, in addition, the balance is back, he may strike his head on the board as he skids.

B) CONTACT AT SURFACE OF WATER

Factors leading to difficulty at the surface of the water are related to takeoff balance, to body control in flight, and control at the point of entry. Don't jump to the conclusion that entry faults are caused by entry techniques alone, but try to perceive the point at which the dive goes out of control. A very flat takeoff, one with very little rotation whatever the dive direction, will lead to a shallow or flat entry. Misjudging the dive break, as in spins, may also result in a flat entry. The slap and stings resulting from these entries produce redness, minor contusions, certainly discomfort, but rarely real injury. From boards higher than one meter, broken blood vessels and more serious internal damage may occur, especially if the diver keeps repeating his fault and hits many times in the same place. Occasional black eyes and bloody noses occur. A rare mishap in incompleted twisting dives is a direct ear slap which can be serious.

More common and harder to prevent are the overthrows from leaning forward on takeoff and/or from lack of body tension in flight, increasing the impact stress on joints. Back strains, neck difficulties, and shoulder problems are injuries from the type of entry in which part of the body is stopped by the impact and part keeps on going in the direction of rotation. This type of entry can also be caused by desperate efforts to save a dive which is going over by a strong pull in the opposing direction. Simply failing to check and stretch at the entry can cause trouble in these joint areas, particularly from boards higher than one meter.

A point to note, so basic that it can be overlooked, is whether the student's eyes are open. It is surprising how many beginners close them tightly at takeoff, and fly through space on complete guesswork. With a little experience a teacher can usually tell when the diver's eyes are closed (or not really being used for aim) even when the teacher is not in a position to see the eyes themselves. Those eyes-closed dives have an uncontrolled "blind" look about them!

C) CONTACT WITH BOTTOM

Once under water the diver must hold his position. Relaxing tension too soon, trying to come to the surface before momentum is spent or a controlled landing is made on the bottom causes similar injuries to overthrow strains at the entry point. Watch the underwater path of the diver for signs of these things. Back position, leg tension, and arm alignment are the major points. If the arms separate too widely under water or drop under the body, the head is vulnerable to hitting bottom. The landing impact should be controlled by the arms and shoulders directly below the total body weight (see p. 36) or by the feet and legs in the case of foot first entries. Ask the diver how he hits the bottom—how hard and in what position.

Though not related to observation of movement patterns, the most frequent cause of accidents on the bottom of the pool is actually unfamiliarity with depths. This means not only the danger of an exceptionally shallow situation but also the adjustment to *any* shallower depth after diving in deeper water. Much care must be taken that the diver not only knows how deep the water is, but also realizes the adjustment he must make in relation to his immediately previous depth experience. Adjustment to depth is a time interval accommodation which can be set very soon if the diver experiments with caution on his first few dives in the new environment. If the contrast from deep to shallow is considerable, it is wise to have the student try some surface dives (head first and foot first) at the approximate point of entry. By these he gets a feeling of measuring his own height (with arms overhead) in the depth of water into which he will be diving. He also ascertains the type of surface on which he will be landing. Several surface dives, plus a few fall-ins from the board, should re-set his time interval expectation.

Another specific problem at the bottom is the effect of water pressure in deep areas. Individuals differ in pressure tolerance on head, ears, and sinuses. Those who are sensitive to pressure should work with surface dives from shallow to deep water to test their tolerance and gradually accustom themselves to greater pressure. Instruction in compensating breath control should be learned, the procedure being to create exhalation pressure without actually blowing out. This will create internal pressure on the ear drum through the Eustachian tube, and if controlled, can negate the increased water pressure on the outside of the ear drum. Extreme cases of sensitivity to water pressure should be advised to stay away from diving.

GENERAL TEACHING RELATING TO ACCIDENT PREVENTION

Many of these factors of potential accident seem far away from the beginning diver. Yet early habits in takeoff balance, control in the air, entry tension, and control in hitting bottom are very important in the long run. The bad habits are most important to correct *early* before they become ingrained habits. Sooner or later the student is going to be diving with more height and cleaner entries. The better he gets the harder he will hit both surface and bottom.

The situations discussed above are trouble spots. While there are many ramifications possible, those are the key points. As a teacher there are many other considerations for you to think about which can have direct bearing on the safety of your students. Beware pushing them beyond control for the sake of new dives. Teach safely within the limits of your own evaluation of the student. Nothing can be gained by pushing beyond safety: if there is not physical injury, there is certainly psychological setback.

Watch for those who have more courage than common sense, particularly those who practice a good deal by themselves. Learn to judge signs of fatigue, such as unusual balking or knees buckling at takeoff. Extreme fear can cause aberrations which are dangerous and unpredictable. In spite of all this cautiousness, you must have the courage to take a chance, backed by everything you know of the student's ability and reactions, every time a new dive is attempted.

One final variable is the general health of the diver. Returning to workouts or even class instruction from illness or from a long layoff, the diver will be unstable and will tire easily. Ask questions occasionally about outside problems which may cause extra tensions or fatigue. Check eating habits, and, most particularly, hours of sleep. To dive on very little sleep, whether a chronic condition or a one night loss, is to take all kinds of chances. Your pace of teaching and severity of discipline must be tempered by all of these considerations if you are to teach safely and successfully.

Index

Index